Enterprising Minnesotans

Enterprising Minnesotans

150 Years of Business Pioneers

Stephen George

Foreword by Marilyn Carlson Nelson

Published in cooperation with the Center for Entrepreneurial Studies
at the Carlson School of Management, University of Minnesota

University of Minnesota Press
Minneapolis — London

This book is dedicated to Minnesota's ultra entrepreneur, Curtis L. Carlson, and his family in heartfelt appreciation for generous financial assistance toward its publication through memorial gifts provided to the University of Minnesota's Curtis L. Carlson School of Management after Mr. Carlson's death in 1999.

Published by the University of Minnesota Press
111 Third Avenue South, Suite 290
Minneapolis, MN 55401-2520
http://www.upress.umn.edu

Library of Congress Cataloging-in-Publication Data

George, Stephen, 1948–
    Enterprising Minnesotans : 150 years of business pioneers / Stephen George.
        p.   cm.
    "Published in cooperation with the Center for Entrepreneurial Studies at the Carlson School of Management, University of Minnesota."
    Includes bibliographical references and index.
    ISBN 0-8166-4219-2 (HC/j : alk. paper)
    1. Businesspeople—United States—Biography.   2. Businesspeople—Minnesota—Biography.   3. Industries—United States—History.   4. Industries—Minnesota—History.
5. Entrepreneurship—United States—History.   6. Entrepreneurship—Minnesota—History.   7. Minnesota—Biography.   I. Center for Entrepreneurial Studies (Carlson School of Management)   II. Title.
    HC102.5.A2 G46 2003
    338.09776'092'2—dc21

                                                                        2002152511

Printed in the United States of America on acid-free paper

The University of Minnesota is an equal-opportunity educator and employer.

12 11 10 09 08 07 06 05 04 03   10 9 8 7 6 5 4 3 2 1

Whatever you can do, or dream you can, begin it!
Boldness has genius, power, and magic in it.

—Johann Wolfgang von Goethe

Contents

Foreword

Marilyn Carlson Nelson

Chair and CEO, Carlson Companies

The ancient Greeks, who seemingly had a saying for everything, said, "A people are known by the heroes they crown." In other words, "Tell me who you admire, and I'll tell you who you are." It's a saying especially appropriate for a book about enterprising Minnesotans.

In *Enterprising Minnesotans,* Stephen George has collected the essence of Minnesota—the unflagging spirit, the sense of community, the crystal-clear vision of the future that have been the hallmark of those who have formed the business and social fabric of our state.

What is it about this place that produces so many visionaries with a drive for success? How did Minneapolis develop to become a city that, along with St. Paul, has nurtured such a disproportionate number of headquarters of so many Fortune 500 corporations? Perhaps it's the short roots that connect the past and current population to the immigrants who ventured into the interior of our great nation, seeking freedom and capital. They were frugal and practical people who saw value in investing in their companies and communities, but no value in things transitory and impermanent. Minnesota humorist Garrison Keillor captures this essence in his imaginary sojourns to Lake Wobegon—where upright citizens brook no waste or nonsense, but are not without their own inventiveness or humor.

I've lived it personally, growing up in a family only one generation off the ship from Sweden. Our family's company was like a sibling to me, and the machinations of business were eagerly taught at our table. More than once my father, who founded the Gold Bond Stamp Company on $55 of defrayed rent and a dream, explained that we could either take a vacation or reinvest that quarter's profit back into our company. We would always vote for vacation, but somehow reinvestment won.

Even into the adult years of my life, the lessons of frugality were taught. Often, after my father drove by my house at night on the way to his own, I would receive a call from him, inquiring, "Are you having a party over there tonight?" That was his way of asking why I had so many lights burning throughout the house. Yet this was a man who built something from nothing and could go to work the next day and gamble millions on a new business venture. It's an illustration of the Minnesota value system at work—don't waste, but invest in that which could turn out to be important someday.

Many of the people who built new lives in Minnesota were Germans and Swedes, by any measure two of the most industrious groups of people you will find. It's no wonder, then, that an old Swedish maxim has taken hold here: "Work all you can. Earn all you can. Give all you can." As you read about enterprising Minnesotans and connect the names to some of the great corporate institutions of our state and nation, you'll start to see a thread. I believe it's one unique to our state and largely responsible for the inordinate level of success its citizens have achieved. It has to do with giving back.

In the 1960s, when the Great Society was beginning to take shape, more and more people began to look toward the government for financial support. During one meeting that Minnesota business leaders had with President Lyndon Johnson, the architect of growing government largesse, the president noted that although government allowed businesses to deduct up to 5 percent of the pretax profits from their annual tax obligation, few businesses were doing so. That was a cue for some of the assembled leaders, who then and there decided to form the Five Percent Club to donate that amount to community causes.

Today the tradition continues in a successor organization, the Keystone Club, and Minnesota business continues to give back. Why? What does Minnesota business get for its money? Simply put: a future.

It is community assets that attract leaders and companies. Good schools, the arts, parks and public spaces, and a strong social safety net are what hold a business community together by providing a strong foundation for families to live and grow. These things attract leaders, who bring their companies to a place far north of anyone's typical radar screen. I believe that it is the immigrant society–born tradition of building community and investing in that which is lasting that is behind the unusual success of our state.

But there is another element as well: faith. Be it faith in a dream, faith in the future, or faith in God, those who have succeeded here have all had a faith in something larger than themselves or the here and now. That is another Minnesota trait.

This book was commissioned to capture the stories of many of Minnesota's most successful entrepreneurs and examine them to uncover the unifying truths of Minnesota success and entrepreneurism. It's supremely appropriate that this book was published in cooperation with the Carlson School of Management at the University of Minnesota, a business school named for my father and devoted to teaching the lessons of business success—and in doing so becoming a crucible for the entrepreneurs of tomorrow.

No mention of the Carlson School of Management would be appropriate without an accompanying mention of Dean David Kidwell, the "father" of the current school. As former University of Minnesota president Mark Yudof said at Dean Kidwell's retirement in 2001 after ten years of service, "David built the Carlson School, both literally and figuratively. Many of the elements associated with the school originated under Dean Kidwell's leadership, including the new building, experiential learning initiatives, and the many international programs now offered."

Also to be saluted is the current dean, Larry Benveniste, who is continuing the tradition of excellence at the school and building on the high quality of teaching and scholarship that has resulted in the Carlson School's moving steadily into the top ranks of the nation's business schools.

As you walk with the entrepreneurs and enterprising souls in this book, I hope you'll come to understand the nature of success better and more deeply, as have I. It's an enjoyable journey through an unusual landscape of personal success that is unique in our country, and perhaps the world.

Acknowledgments

Enterprising Minnesotans: 150 Years of Business Pioneers was commissioned by the Center for Entrepreneurial Studies at the University of Minnesota's Carlson School of Management. Doug Johnson, codirector of the center, established the book's vision and scope while Lois Graham, the center's associate administrator, managed the project and provided unwavering support. Writers relish such complete support and encouragement, and I want to thank Doug and Lois for bringing me into this rewarding project.

The research required for this book led me to ask many companies for information and photographs. The people who responded were always willing to send me what I needed, and I thank them for taking time from their already busy days to help me.

I especially would like to thank the librarians and staff at the Minnesota Historical Society for their resources and guidance. Many of the interesting stories in this book came from the archives at the Minnesota History Center, and more than half of the book's photographs were found in its visual database.

Ellen Carroll George accompanied me on several trips to the history center and helped me track down the bits and pieces of information needed to create a book. Ellen enjoys finding that elusive fact or photograph; her love of research, of books, and of the buildings that house them has contributed to her fine assistance on this project, and I greatly appreciate her work.

As always, I thank Ellen and my children, Dan, Katie, Allie, and Zack, for their love and support.

Prologue

At the beginning of the 2001 Toys for Tots campaign, a representative of Best Buy appeared on a Twin Cities television news program to hand over a check for $250,000. The meteorologist who accepted the electronics superstore's gift on behalf of the charity seemed stunned by the sum, and the news anchors wondered aloud if the annual campaign had ever received such an enormous single donation. A delegate from the national Toys for Tots program provided perspective by pointing out that, in 2000, citizens and companies in the Twin Cities area contributed one toy of every twenty-five collected nationally by 350 such programs.

In fact, Minnesota has long been a leader in charitable contributions. Its companies and citizens—including Best Buy's Richard Schulze, one of more than forty Minnesota entrepreneurs featured in this book—have inherited a tradition of giving that can be traced to entrepreneurial legends such as Charles A. Pillsbury, James J. Hill, Frederick Weyerhaeuser, George Draper Dayton, William McKnight, and Hans Andersen.

Enterprising Minnesotans tells the stories of the men and women throughout Minnesota's rich history who have created exceptional organizations. Some survived high adventure to endure, recovering financially from a devastating explosion (Cadwallader Washburn), seizing opportunities during an economic panic (Will Cargill), or avoiding death from freezing or sliding off the road (Carl Wickman). Others overcame seemingly endless setbacks to discover iron ore (Leonidas Merritt), move lumber to market more efficiently (Frederick Weyerhaeuser), or introduce a radical medical treatment (Sister Elizabeth Kenny). Many jumped from business to business before settling on the one that would realize their dreams.

What these entrepreneurs have done best is transform dreams into enduring enterprises. *Enterprising Minnesotans* tells their fascinating stories of incredible triumph and tragedy, exceptional abilities to overcome adversity, unwavering confidence, bold decisions, and tenacity that often defied reasonable thinking. Most have been white men, especially early in the state's history, because white men at that time dominated government and commerce to the exclusion of women and people of other races. While this skews the diversity represented in the book, the overarching goal of this project is to feature entrepreneurs who established companies that continue to excel today.

In every case but one, the featured entrepreneurs built organizations that outlived them. This impressive list includes Cargill, General Mills, Mayo Clinic, Andersen Corporation, Carlson Companies, Medtronic, and Best Buy. Some notable Minnesota companies are not included, not because they have been less successful but because they landed farther down the list according to very subjective criteria. When choosing among enduring enterprises to spotlight in each of five major periods in Minnesota's history, my criteria in order of priority were as follows.

1. *Quality of the story.* A primary goal of this book is to share the experiences of successful Minnesota entrepreneurs. In some cases, a founder's story is little more than a collection of key events that gives no connection to or sense of the person behind them. In other cases, it's not clear who among several candidates actually got the business going. Stories in this book focus on the people responsible for establishing enduring enterprises.

2. *Significance of the company.* All but one of the entrepreneurs featured in this book began companies that have endured; the exception is Leonidas Merritt, whose operation with his brothers, Mountain Iron Company, lasted less than four years. Yet their story is instructive both in how they ushered in an important industry for Minnesota and in how they lost everything in such a short time. Another caveat: the more recently a company was started, the less time it has had to establish itself as enduring. In these rapidly changing times, when even the giants of industry must reinvent themselves, no company can claim permanent significance.

3. *Diversity.* As much as possible, once the quality of the story and the significance of the company had been determined, the focus turned to including a diversity of entrepreneurs, industries, and regions of Minnesota.

Although the entrepreneurs who met these criteria often exhibited similar characteristics, no single pattern emerges. Some were charismatic leaders, others more methodical managers. Some reveled in the spotlight; others avoided it. Some assumed great personal and professional risk, and others sought steadier growth. Some were experts in their field, while others were expert entrepreneurs who hired people with the knowledge they needed.

One of the most interesting differences is how some created enduring enterprises by intent, while others fell into them by accident. George Draper Dayton never intended to be a retailer, for example, but when he took over a department store because those running it couldn't pay the rent, he invested all the knowledge and energy he could muster into making it work. "Success in any department of life," he wrote, "is attained only through ceaseless industry and careful thinking."

Dayton's motto summarizes common traits of the entrepreneurs in this book, and successful entrepreneurs in any era: their ability to conquer new frontiers through hard work and innovative thinking. And there are always new frontiers. Whether prospectors stake claims in a wilderness stream or prospective dot-comers stake claims through streaming video, a frontier excites the imagination and involves the senses.

Since it became a U.S. territory in 1849, Minnesota has been home to a diverse group of successful enterprises, from family farms to filling stations, banks to bakeries, grocery stores to medical practices to myriad stores that line Main Street in every small town. The men and women who launched these businesses made their living providing goods and services that people were willing to buy. In true entrepreneurial spirit, they chose independence over security, opportunity over peace of mind, and dreams over playing it safe. They made these choices not only because they believed in the promise of their ideas but also because they believed in themselves. They believed they would succeed, and that belief sustained them.

What differentiates the featured entrepreneurs from the hundreds of thousands who have set up shop across Minnesota during the past 150 years is the depth of that belief. Those who have created enduring enterprises moved beyond belief to bold actions few would consider or attempt. Despite frequent setbacks and crushing adversity, they formed valuable new organizations through their imagination, energy, tenacity, and courage.

Enterprising Minnesotans tells their stories.

Pioneering Spirit (1849–1865)

James Madison Goodhue

The first heavy snow of the season fell on the first day of November 1848 in St. Paul, Minnesota, and remained until March. A few days after the snowfall the country elected a president, although the town's nine hundred residents didn't learn who had won until January, because they had no way of getting the election results. The nearest mail-distribution point lay two hundred miles down the frozen Mississippi River in Prairie du Chien, Wisconsin, and when ice locked the river, the citizens of St. Paul were isolated. In January 1849, however, a dogsled driver arrived with two news items: Zachary Taylor had been elected the twelfth president of the United States, but the lobbying of Henry Sibley (a Minnesota delegate to the U.S. Congress who would become the state's first governor) and Henry Rice (a developer and an Indian treaty negotiator who would become Minnesota's first senator) and the support of Illinois senator Stephen A. Douglas had not been enough to make Minnesota a U.S. territory. St. Paulites would have to wait until the first steamboat arrived on April 9 to celebrate the news that territorial status had finally been achieved.

Nine days later, on April 18, another steamboat docked in St. Paul, but instead of carrying outstanding news, it carried an outstanding newsman: James Madison Goodhue. Goodhue believed that the territorial government to be established in St. Paul would open a new frontier and create opportunities for a pioneer journalist, and, at the age of thirty-nine, with experience as a farmer, lawyer, and newspaper publisher, he relished the challenge.

Less than two weeks later, Goodhue published the first issue of the *Minnesota Pioneer* on the printing press he had brought with him from Lancaster, Wisconsin, and

1

James Madison Goodhue. Painting by Ernest Galvan. Courtesy of the Minnesota Historical Society.

had set up in a rickety building through which, he wrote, "out-of-doors is visible by more than 500 apertures." He had intended to name his paper *The Epistle of St. Paul,* but good sense prevailed. Besides, *Pioneer* accurately captured the spirit of the frontier town. "St. Paul . . . is about as large as a mob on the increase," Goodhue wrote in the *Pioneer* in May. "It looks as if the seeds for a multitude of tenements had been scattered yesterday upon a bed of guano, and had sprouted up into cabins, and stores and sheds and warehouses, fresh from the sawmill, since the last sun shone." The sawmill belonged to Franklin Steele and was strategically located at the falls of St.

Anthony, ten miles up the Mississippi River. Demand forced the mill to run day and night, cutting green pine lumber that builders used without waiting for it to season.

In the same editorial, Goodhue defined the entrepreneurial spirit that drew him, Steele, and others to Minnesota: "Men of the right stamp will always find the right spots; and men of the right *nerve* will stay in them and flourish, regardless of all temporary inconvenience."

It has been more than 150 years since Goodhue so eloquently captured the character of the true entrepreneur, yet his description, like the enterprise he started, has endured. Minnesota's rich heritage of men and women who flourish in the harshest circumstances began when Minnesota was neither a territory nor a state but an American Indian word for the silt-laden water of the Minnesota River. Colonel Josiah Snelling took command of two hundred men in 1820 with a single objective: to build a frontier post where the Minnesota and Mississippi Rivers met. His men cut logs in the Rum River region northwest of St. Paul and floated them to the falls of St. Anthony, where Snelling erected a sawmill. He completed his fort in 1824 and remained in command until 1827, when future U.S. president Zachary Taylor relieved him. Taylor, a southern-born officer, lasted a year, later describing Minnesota as a "most miserable and uninteresting country."

Goodhue disagreed. Contrary to the popular newspaper policy of his day, he published local news rather than rehash national and international events. He demonstrated good business sense by staying close both to his customers and his adopted territory. He kept abreast of local doings by delivering his papers himself, walking the length and breadth of a growing St. Paul, talking with anyone willing to share a story or point him toward a newsworthy source. He also took every opportunity to explore the Minnesota Territory on horseback and by steamboat and canoe, reporting what he discovered in the *Pioneer.*

After St. Paul became the capital of the new Minnesota Territory, steamboats regularly arrived from points south to unload immigrants and merchandise. The stream of people strained the young community's capacity to provide food and shelter. Goodhue warned about the housing shortage in the February 27, 1850, edition of the *Minnesota Pioneer:* "We would advise each immigrant to St. Paul this season, as we did last season, to come here prepared to build a cheap house immediately, without depending upon hiring a house. A rough and ready residence can be erected in a week, at a trifling cost."

Goodhue "was constantly upon the alert to find whatever might contribute to the general prosperity of Minnesota," a friend later said. In his editorials, he frequently called for bridges, railroads, and better roads to serve the growing population. He sent his newspaper east and south to recruit settlers. He even touted the potential of the city's neighbor across the river, the rapidly growing village of St. Anthony—but not without stirring up a friendly rivalry between St. Paul and what would become Minneapolis that continues to this day.

In 1850 the city of Minneapolis did not yet exist, for the land west of the Mississippi River had not been settled and was still the domain of American Indians. St. Anthony,

Goodhue's newspaper office on the southeast corner of Third and Jackson Streets in St. Paul.
Photograph courtesy of the Minnesota Historical Society.

on the east side of the falls, had been a natural meeting place for fur traders who had to portage around the waterfall. Although Franklin Steele had tapped into that water-power for his sawmill, St. Anthony had not yet attracted the people or the attention of its sister city to the southeast.

Some of its residents, however, boasted that the city by the falls would some-day surpass the size and scope of St. Paul. Goodhue grudgingly acknowledged the possibility: "We do not say that St. Paul will always be the most important town in Minnesota," he wrote, "and we do not say that St. Anthony will *not* be." At the same time, he took every opportunity to needle the folks at St. Anthony about the gap between their expectations and reality. In 1850, he wrote, "There was a notable fire in St. Anthony last Tuesday. It was indeed an important conflagration. The flames swept across vast open spaces whereon it is expected that some day mammoth costly struc-tures will stand, and if they had only been there the other day enormous would have been the loss to the 'metropolis of the Northwest.'"

Goodhue's sense of humor permeated the *Pioneer,* ranging from the sarcastic to the fanciful. He wrote editorials on Sunday after breakfast, sitting at his desk with his hat on, shoulders shaking as he laughed at his own cleverness. He once advertised a race at a specific date and time between a feeble steamboat that always struggled against the current and a sawmill standing below town. People congregated on the shore for the sheer silliness of the moment.

Looking west across the Mississippi River from St. Anthony to the new village of Minneapolis in 1855. Photograph by F. M. Laraway. Courtesy of the Minnesota Historical Society.

St. Paul in 1857, with the young state's first capitol building in the center. Photograph by B. F. Upton. Courtesy of the Minnesota Historical Society.

Goodhue's humor did not always serve him well. When it became apparent that the United States would purchase the land west of the Mississippi, people wondered what to call the new town sure to spring up across the river from St. Anthony. In keeping with the practice of the day, many proposed naming it after a favorite saint. Goodhue suggested they call it All Saints "so as to head off the whole calendar of saints." The people of St. Anthony, including its most influential citizens, felt Goodhue was mocking them. When he subsequently applied to be the public printer for the territory, a plum job that promised a steadier income, he lost his bid because of the protests of those he had offended. And it wasn't just his humor that riled. In 1851, after writing a scathing editorial, Goodhue was attacked and stabbed twice. He shot his assailant. Both men survived, although Goodhue died a year-and-a-half later from infections caused by the stabbing. The *Pioneer* merged with the *St. Paul Press* in 1861 and became the *St. Paul Pioneer Press.*

Goodhue's stabbing reflected the frontier mentality of Minnesota's early days, when entrepreneurs were truly pioneers. Most settlers came from the eastern United States, although a few French Canadians still plied the fur trade. Winters were harsh, the cold and snow isolating those hardy enough to make the new territory their home. The lack of reliable, consistent transportation to the outside world, together with the still small population, limited the potential of any business to reach enough customers to survive. Those who did survive not only offered a product that appealed to

East-side dam in the Mississippi River at St. Anthony Falls around 1860. Photograph courtesy of the Minnesota Historical Society.

a large percentage of the available market, but they also sought ways to expand, as Goodhue did by distributing his newspaper to other parts of the country to attract new settlers—and new customers—to St. Paul.

Yet even this was rarely enough to provide financial security, which is why so many early entrepreneurs pursued so many different endeavors. Goodhue stretched his entrepreneurial muscles by investing in real estate and running a ferry across the Mississippi. One of Minnesota's greatest entrepreneurs, James J. Hill, worked for a steamboat company, pressed and sold hay, served as a warehouseman, and ran a coal-fuel business. He was involved in the stock market, banking, international trade, and mining during the time he built his railroad. He also shared Goodhue's desire to promote the growth of the new frontier, sending agents to Europe to show slides of Minnesota farming and offering cheap railroad tickets to immigrants who settled along the route. Another prominent Minnesota entrepreneur, George Draper Dayton, owned a lumberyard before opening a loan and investment company. He bought a flour mill, traded it for land, then traded the land for property upon which he constructed a building that became the site of his most successful and unexpected venture, the Dayton's department store.

Jane Grey Swisshelm

While many of Minnesota's early entrepreneurs followed opportunities far afield from their original areas of expertise, a few stuck to what they knew. Take the newspaper business, for example. A few years after Goodhue antagonized the citizens of St. Anthony, Jane Grey Swisshelm began agitating the people of St. Cloud, a town northwest of St. Paul along the Mississippi River. A pioneer journalist who had been the first woman to sit in the Senate press gallery, Swisshelm left Pittsburgh to become the owner and editor of the *St. Cloud Visiter* in 1858 (the spelling was a tribute to Samuel Johnson, who contributed to a monthly publication called the *Universal Visiter*). Like Goodhue, she was an opinionated writer, arguing endlessly for women's rights and against slavery. In almost every issue of her paper, she wrote: "Paying taxes is as unwomanly as voting; and is a privilege which should be exclusively confined to 'white male citizens, of this and other countries,' until women share with them the responsibility of saying what shall be done with the money they are required to contribute to the public treasury."

Her strong opinions stirred up strong resentment. One night someone broke into her newspaper office, wrecked the printing press, and dumped cases of type into the river. Incensed, Swisshelm presented her thoughts about the culprits in her paper. Prominent citizens accused her of libel. Compromising to avoid legal hassles, she promised to stop attacking the good citizens of St. Cloud in the *Visiter*. True to her word, the next week her attacks appeared in her new paper, the *St. Cloud Democrat*.

After the outbreak of the Civil War, Swisshelm sold the newspaper and worked as a nurse for the Union Army. She sent angry letters to the St. Cloud paper about the conditions in military hospitals. When the war ended, she retired to Swissvale, Pennsylvania, to write her autobiography. She died in 1884 at the age of sixty-eight.

Jane Grey Swisshelm. Photograph courtesy of the Minnesota Historical Society.

In the nine years between Goodhue starting his newspaper and Swisshelm running hers, the population of the Minnesota Territory jumped from 6,000 to more than 150,000. By 1890 Minnesota's population approached 1.3 million. Such explosive growth helped create the golden age of entrepreneurship in Minnesota, as we will see in the next chapter. It also opened doors to many who had been unable to enter the white-dominated business world, such as journalist John Quincy Adams.

John Quincy Adams

Of the fourteen "black newspapers" started in the Twin Cities between 1885 and 1919, the most senior was the *Appeal*, which became, under the leadership of African

John Quincy Adams. Photograph courtesy of the Minnesota Historical Society.

American John Quincy Adams, one of the country's most prominent such papers. Adams served as the *Appeal*'s editor from 1886 until his death in 1921, and his career paved the way for today's *Minnesota Spokesman-Recorder* while providing opportunities for young people, such as Twin Cities civil rights leader Roy Wilkins. Although the *Appeal* was never very profitable, it played a critical role in binding the Twin Cities' African American communities and connecting them with others nationwide.

Establishing connections ranks high among a visionary entrepreneur's skills. In some cases, such as Hill's railroad, the connection is a physical link between communities and markets. In others, such as the logging enterprises of Frederick Weyerhaeuser, Hill's neighbor and one of the country's greatest lumbermen, the connection involves uniting people with a common interest—in his case, the desire to mill timber more efficiently.

In fact, one of the distinguishing characteristics of most of the entrepreneurs featured in this book is their ability to see connections that others either miss or dismiss. When Joel Ronning saw the connection between the Internet and the distribution of products, for example, he founded Digital River to help software companies deliver their products over the Internet.

Story after story shows how these entrepreneurs made connections that others overlooked. They recognized an emerging market. They saw the potential of a promising technology. They understood the opportunities of a glaring need. They imagined a new world order in an emerging perspective. Most important, they acted on their discoveries despite the skepticism of their peers and the tenuous nature of their ideas.

Consider the number of entrepreneurs whose ideas were publicly demeaned as folly: Cadwallader Washburn's first Minneapolis flour mill, Frank Peavey's concrete grain silo, and Hill's railroad to the Pacific, to name a few. Standing up to public ridicule—and the real possibility of public failure—required remarkable self-confidence, especially when those taking the risks were rarely experts in their chosen fields.

Washburn knew nothing about flour milling when he started his company, nor did his chief competitor, Charles Pillsbury. Theodore Hamm understood raising and butchering cattle and continued to supply meat to the people of St. Paul long after he hired an expert to run his new brewery. J. A. O. Preus became the commissioner of insurance for Minnesota despite having no experience in the area, but the knowledge he gained helped get Lutheran Brotherhood off the ground. Colonel Lewis Brittin designed and managed a central terminal that combined the facilities of local railroads; that he lacked any knowledge about running an airline didn't prevent him from founding Northwest Airways.

Not every entrepreneur featured in this book started enterprises they knew nothing about. James Madison Goodhue, for example, had owned and published a newspaper before starting the *Minnesota Pioneer*. What the stories of these entrepreneurs reveal is that expertise in a business did not predict success any more than a lack of expertise prevented it.

Alexander Wilkin

Many successful entrepreneurs knew just enough about a business to recognize an opportunity others had missed. Alexander Wilkin arrived in St. Paul from New York in the early summer of 1849, two months after Goodhue printed the first issue of his newspaper. Wilkin was a scrappy little fellow, all of five-foot-one and one hundred pounds, an infantry captain in the Mexican War as well as a lawyer and politician.

Alexander Wilkin. Engraving courtesy of The St. Paul Companies Archives.

By August, the thirty-year-old participated in the first court session in the Minnesota Territory, and soon had influential people in and outside of the territory send letters to President Taylor urging him to appoint Wilkin secretary of the territory. When Taylor died in office after serving less than a year, Millard Fillmore, his successor, made the appointment.

Like other entrepreneurs of his time, Wilkin acted upon nearly every opportunity that presented itself. In addition to being territorial secretary and a practicing lawyer, at one time during the 1850s he was a federal marshal, newspaper publisher, land developer, real estate agent, and insurance-company representative. By the end of 1852 he had parlayed his real estate business into a net worth of $15,000. Locals claimed that, at one time, he owned half of St. Paul.

Wilkin's experience as an agent for eastern insurance companies convinced him of the potential for a local fire and marine insurance company. Optimism has rarely been so irrational, for Wilkin aspired to sell fire insurance in a pioneer town full of wooden structures that was still a year away from having a fire department. Nonetheless, in 1853 he became one of the originators and the first president of the St. Paul Mutual Insurance Company, which he based in his law office. The company's incorporators included many of the territory's leading citizens: Auguste Larpenteur, a store owner and one of St. Paul's earliest settlers; Charles Borup, a fur trader and banker; Governor Alexander Ramsey; and Henry Rice.

It was a precipitous time in Minnesota history: First, in 1853 a treaty with American Indians opened the land west of the Mississippi River to settlers. Second, the following February the railroad extended its track west to Rock Island, Illinois, making it possible for immigrants to take the train to Rock Island, then hop a Mississippi River steamboat to Minnesota. The pivotal events drew speculators to St. Paul to cash in on what they believed would be the next great midwestern city. Wilkin wrote his father, "This is now the great point in the Country to which the eyes of speculators are turned and property will go up as it did at the same period in the history of Chicago and St. Louis; but look out for a similar crash in a year or two more."

His prediction proved correct, although it took a little longer than he anticipated. The crash of 1857 was characterized by plunging real-estate values and countless bankruptcies and foreclosures. Banks closed their doors. Little money circulated. Improvements ceased. Fewer than 20 percent of businesses survived. Typical of financial panics, the economy had been based on the promise of future growth rather than sound economic sense. The population of St. Paul shriveled to half what it had been before the panic, and a general gloom prevailed until business began to pick up again in 1860.

The panic of 1857 wiped out forty-seven mutual insurance companies, but the St. Paul Mutual Insurance Company survived. Wilkin closed the books to new business and sold most of his office furniture. His actions saved the company, which remained solvent with a balance of $80, although it would not resume selling insurance until after the Civil War, when it was reincorporated as a stock company under a new name, the St. Paul Fire and Marine Insurance Company.

The St. Paul Fire and Marine office tucked into the Merchants Hotel in St. Paul. Photograph courtesy of The St. Paul Companies Archives.

Unfortunately, it resumed without Wilkin, whose military experience elevated him to captain of Company A of the First Minnesota Infantry Regiment. He was killed in Mississippi in 1864 at the Battle of Tupelo.

James Madison Goodhue never lived to see the birth of a new city west of St. Anthony, dying in 1852. The deaths of Goodhue and Wilkin suggest the perilous times these early entrepreneurs faced. It is hard to imagine how pioneering Minnesotans survived each winter, much less the poor transportation, relative isolation, and erratic law enforcement. An uncertain political future also plagued the territory for much of the 1850s as it sought statehood.

A convention in Stillwater on August 26, 1848, called on President James Polk to establish the Minnesota Territory. Iowa had tried to extend its northern boundary all the way to Brainerd, Minnesota, but a congressional committee led by Stephen A. Douglas, who later lost the 1860 presidential race to Abraham Lincoln, fixed Iowa's current northern boundary. Wisconsin entered the fray by proposing a western boundary that would have included St. Paul, but it was rebuffed as well. Thanks to the lobbying efforts of Henry Sibley and Henry Rice, Polk signed into law the bill that created the territory of Minnesota on March 3, 1849. Two days later Zachary Taylor became president. He offered the governorship of the new territory to men from Missouri, Indiana, and New Jersey, but they all declined. His fourth choice, thirty-four-year-old Alexander Ramsey of Pennsylvania, accepted, but was defeated by Henry Sibley in 1857 before winning the governorship in 1859.

While today's entrepreneurs seek to carve out new territory in a business or industry, these early entrepreneurs had to carve out part of a country while establishing their companies. By the time Minnesota became the thirty-second state in 1858, they had laid the foundation for its rapid growth. By 1858, sixty-two steamboats made regular trips to St. Paul from the end of the railroad line in Rock Island, Illinois, carrying German, Norwegian, and other immigrants seeking good farming land. Fort Ridgely, on the Minnesota River near the present-day city of New Ulm, reported 394 steamboat landings in 1858 alone. The new state benefited from two major nineteenth-century events: the westward movement from Europe to the United States and an internal westward movement within the United States. Early Minnesotans such as Goodhue, Wilkin, Washburn, Sibley, and Rice came mainly from New England and New York. Seven of the state's first ten governors were New Englanders.

Although a few companies featured in this book got their start in other states, all established their headquarters in Minnesota. Will Cargill bought his first grain elevator in Iowa, for example, while Frederick Weyerhaeuser launched his lumber empire in Wisconsin. Cadwallader Washburn, the man largely responsible for Minnesota's flour-milling legacy, lived in Madison as the governor of Wisconsin at the same time his company produced Gold Medal flour in Minneapolis. These remarkable men were the exceptions; most of the entrepreneurs profiled in these pages lived and worked in Minnesota. Consider Alexander Hartman, founder of the Duluth Electric Company.

Alexander Hartman

At the age of twenty-four, Alexander Hartman supervised more than two hundred men working on the Lake Superior section of the Northern Pacific Railway near the port city of Duluth, Minnesota. The year was 1888. Restless to run his own business and realizing that the steady growth of Duluth promised an attractive market for electricity, the native Minnesotan, born in Shakopee in 1864, started the Duluth Electric Company using boilers and generators from a burned-out grain elevator.

At the time, few limits on the incorporation of utilities produced intense competition. Hartman used a series of reorganizations to survive a lack of capital until he was able to secure a half-million-dollar loan in 1893, thanks mainly to the discovery of iron ore on the Mesabi Range.

Hartman survived and thrived through imagination, energy, tenacity, and courage. "In thinking over the years gone by," he said after his business was established, "I have found that many of the things we fear almost never happen. In my long experience, though things often looked very dark, we always seemed to pull through somehow and come forth triumphantly. And so there is no need to lose our courage—and remember *never* to lose your sense of humor."

James Madison Goodhue could not have said it better.

Alexander Hartman. Photograph courtesy of the Northeast Minnesota Historical Center.

Betting on the Future (1865–1890)

Frederick Weyerhaeuser

When the railroad reached Rock Island, Illinois, in 1854, its owners decided to promote the new line with an event they called "the Great Railroad Excursion." They invited hundreds of guests, including former U.S. president Millard Fillmore (who had named Alexander Wilkin secretary of the Minnesota Territory and whose half-brother helped Wilkin start the St. Paul Mutual Insurance Company), to discover the frontier now within easy reach because of the railroad. The guests took the train from points east to Rock Island before boarding a steamboat for St. Paul.

Few took better advantage of this new connection than a German lad named Frederick Weyerhaeuser. Born in Germany's Rhine Valley in 1834, he quit school when he was thirteen, farmed for his father until his father's death, then immigrated to Pennsylvania, where he worked in a brewery for two years. He decided not to make his career in brewing, he said, "when I saw how often brewers became their own best customers." In 1856, with a little money his father had left him, he took the train to the end of the line, intent on farming near Rock Island. But first, he got a job at a local sawmill.

Weyerhaeuser worked hard and saved his money. At the age of twenty-one he showed surprising initiative by selling lumber to an eager customer for $60 in gold even though he had been given no authority to make such a deal. The mill owners appreciated his gumption. Within months he was managing the mill, then the owners' lumberyard, in the nearby town of Coal Valley.

The company failed following the panic of 1857. A relative of the senior partner who had lent the company money persuaded Weyerhaeuser to buy the lumberyard

Frederick Weyerhaeuser. Photograph from *Timber and Men: The Weyerhaeuser Story,* by Ralph Hidy, Frank Hill, and Allan Nevins (1963). Courtesy of the Minnesota Historical Society.

and assume its debt. Since there was little money in circulation at the time, he built barns and houses in exchange for livestock, which he then traded for logs that he ran through the Rock Island mill to make lumber to build more barns and houses. In two years he made $8,000.

While making a profit during an economic downturn is admirable, Weyerhaeuser's achievement is even more impressive considering his inexperience and his natural shyness, in part because of his strong German accent. He was new to the country, new to the community, and new to the business, but he overcame these obstacles through hard work, thrift, and a keen eye for the future of an industry he would eventually help shape, first in Illinois, then in Wisconsin and Minnesota, and last in Washington and Oregon.

In Minnesota's frontier days, economic diversity and growth came from its three great natural resources: forests, fertile soil, and iron ore. Of the three, timber set the table, making economic growth possible by bringing loggers and their families to the territory, spawning sawmills and lumberyards, attracting secondary businesses to support the growth, and generating the capital and business experience new industries required. Without the lumber industry, Minneapolis would have lacked the capital to finance new flour mills, which in turn inspired farmers to grow wheat, which encouraged railroad owners to lay track throughout the state, which opened national markets for Minnesota's agricultural and mining products.

The most coveted timber in Minnesota was the white pine found in every county east of the Mississippi. Loggers sought white pine because its lightness allowed it to float down streams when hardwoods sank. Sawmill operators liked it because it was soft and straight-grained. Builders preferred pine because it was strong, durable, and abundant. The richest stands extended from Duluth southwest to the Snake River, west to Mille Lacs, then north along the Mississippi River to Leech Lake. When the Indian treaties of 1837 made these stands available to loggers, the trees they found were often 100 feet tall, with some reaching 150 feet. The lumber from these pine forests would be used to build Minneapolis and St. Paul and the smaller towns of Minnesota, as well as Omaha, Kansas City, Des Moines, Topeka, and many other midwestern cities.

In 1864 Frederick Weyerhaeuser bought his first timber in upper Wisconsin along the Chippewa River. Using money he had saved, he planned to control a steady supply of logs for his Illinois sawmill and lumberyard. He also remembered the strict forest-conservation laws in his native Germany and expected that the time would come when America's abundant lumber supply would shrink, making his investment more valuable. What he did not anticipate was how hard it would be just to get his logs to his mill.

In those days, loggers cut timber during the winter, dragging the logs over the snow with teams of oxen. In the spring they marked their logs for identification. Another company drove the logs down the tributary rivers to the Mississippi, where a different company took over rafting them down the river. Yet another company acted as log broker. Along the way, logs were sold to the first sawmill ready to buy, creating logjams at Eau Claire and Chippewa Falls, Wisconsin, as raftsmen sorted through the logs to find those with a particular mark. Mills farther down the river, like Weyerhaeuser's, had to wait a long time to get their wood.

Weyerhaeuser (second from right) regularly assessed the value of the timber in his Wisconsin holdings. Photograph from *Timber and Men: The Weyerhaeuser Story.* Courtesy of the Minnesota Historical Society.

To Weyerhaeuser, who hated inefficiency, the whole process begged for a new approach. He started with what he could control, hiring his own people to handle every step, from cutting the logs to rafting them down the river to his sawmill. Seeing the number of logs lost at sandbars and on rocks, he directed his men not to lose a single stick. Next he tackled the two-headed beast causing logjams: the cutthroat competition of rival mill men on both sides of the Mississippi River from Minnesota to Missouri, and the hostility of sawmill owners at Eau Claire and Chippewa Falls who resented the Mississippi mill men for clogging up the Chippewa River.

Weyerhaeuser applied his exceptional skills as a patient negotiator to the first problem. He persuaded the Mississippi mill owners to band together, negotiating behind the scenes for several years to create the Minnesota River Logging Company in 1870. The cooperative enterprise saw immediate benefits from new efficiencies, many of which Weyerhaeuser identified. It used a single brand to identify the cooperative's logs, then began grading all the logs cut by its members so that each could remove the equivalent of what he had put in rather than sort through the logs for a particular brand. The company moved its logs down the Chippewa River to a big backwash where the logs were held until they could be rafted down the Mississippi.

Obstacles still remained on the Chippewa River, where mills continued to delay the movement of logs until they culled theirs from the pack. The Chippewa mill owners appealed to the U.S. district attorney to stop the cooperative from using the back-

Logjams such as this one at Chippewa Falls, Wisconsin, in the spring of 1869 led Weyerhaeuser to create the Mississippi River Logging Company. Photograph by Charles A. Zimmerman. Courtesy of the Minnesota Historical Society.

wash for collecting logs, but lost. They sued the cooperative, claiming its logs threatened navigation on the river, but lost again. At the same time, Weyerhaeuser fought battles with steamboat operators and the Wisconsin legislature. A fierce competitor and tenacious negotiator, he managed to hold off any legislative intervention while assuaging the Chippewa contingent by proposing the formation of a new corporation that would buy all the logs on the river and distribute them fairly to the Chippewa and Mississippi mills. The new alliance, called the Chippewa Logging Company, dominated the area's lumber industry until 1900, when the timber thinned out and the industry moved on.

A consistent strategy guided Weyerhaeuser's activities: locate strategically, invest as little as possible initially, build conservatively, expand broadly, keep a minority interest, reinvest profits, and supervise everything in person. He preferred to manage vast territory rather than own a smaller patch outright. In his multitude of dealings he excelled at networking, forming one partnership after another with whoever wanted in on the action. "The only times I ever lost money," he once said, "were when I didn't buy." Many of his partners had no idea who his other partners were because of the private gentlemen's agreements Weyerhaeuser made.

Although he never sought majority interest in any enterprise, he ran every one of them. By 1900 he was president or de facto head of more than twenty lumber and railroad companies with influence in every part of the country. Like many of the entrepreneurs profiled in this book, Weyerhaeuser paid close attention to detail during his ten- to twelve-hour working days. In the fall he traveled throughout the pine forests, often covering three thousand miles or more, visiting every camp and landing, determining the value of the logs in the pool.

As the available timber in Wisconsin declined, Weyerhaeuser and his counterparts moved west. He built a house on Summit Avenue in St. Paul in 1891 to be closer to the center of his growing empire. His neighbor was James J. Hill, an arrangement that allowed Weyerhaeuser to maintain contact with this crucial ally while retaining a level of obscurity in the shadow of Hill's personality and the mansion he had constructed.

To encourage railroads to develop new territory, the government granted them land. Hill took Weyerhaeuser to Washington State to show him the large stands of Douglas fir, spruce, cedar, and white pine owned by Great Northern Railways. Weyerhaeuser bought nine hundred thousand acres from Hill at a cost of $6 an acre, knowing the land would be worth two or three times that amount in a short time. Within a few years, Weyerhaeuser companies owned two million acres of timberland in the Northwest.

By the time Weyerhaeuser moved to St. Paul, the Twin Cities had become a major metropolitan area, built largely by the lumber and flour-milling industries. Minneapolis grew from just 13,000 people in 1870 to 164,000 in 1890, while St. Paul jumped from 20,000 to 133,000. In 1870, 15 Minneapolis sawmills handled logs cut from land along the Rum and Mississippi Rivers. By 1880 the number of mills had grown to 234 and they were turning out $7.5 million in lumber each year. Minnesota replaced Wisconsin as the nation's chief source of lumber, a trend Weyerhaeuser had anticipated by buying timberland in Minnesota before the large stands in Wisconsin disappeared.

Frederick Weyerhaeuser died in 1914 at the age of eighty. Not only did he shape an industry, he launched a number of enduring enterprises, many of which bear his name, through, as Richard G. Lillard explained in his biographical article "Timber King," "his untiring energy, his keen business insight, his quick grasp of every important factor in submitted propositions, his instant recognition of profitable opportunities, his unerring judgment, and his dispatch of business through a marvelous executive ability."

Despite the rapid growth of the lumber industry, by 1870 flour had surpassed lumber as the top manufactured product in Minneapolis. To understand why—and to gauge the impact of millers such as Cadwallader Washburn and Charles Pillsbury and grain merchants such as Frank Peavey, Will Cargill, and John MacMillan—one must first understand agriculture in Minnesota at the end of the Civil War.

It was early frontier farming. Much of the Minnesota Territory had been open less than a decade and few towns had been laid out before 1855. The great immigration of Scandinavian farmers was still more than a decade away. European pioneers gravitated to the Big Woods that stretched from St. Cloud to Mankato to Northfield, where elm, oak, maple, and other hardwoods soared 100 feet in the air. Settlers had to clear away the trees before they could farm. At first, they grew what would sustain their families through the cold, long winters. As they cleared more land and their productivity improved, they grew wheat as their cash crop because no efficient way existed to separate corn from the cob and oats were too light to transport economically. Wheat had national and international markets.

Farming during the Civil War was a perilous occupation. Cold and floods threatened crops. Upon harvest, a Minnesota farmer often had to travel one hundred miles or more over forest trails and rutted paths, menaced by thieves, to get his wheat to market, with no guarantee of a fair price when he arrived. Fortunately for farmers, the war boosted demand, and Minnesota's wheat harvest doubled between 1860 and 1865 while the price tripled. The demand exposed new opportunities for ambitious entrepreneurs both to transport and store the grain and to mill it into flour.

Cadwallader Washburn and Charles Pillsbury

Cadwallader Washburn was a Maine man, born in 1818, one of eleven children. As a boy he worked on his father's farm, then clerked in a local store and post office. At twenty he tried teaching for a year before deciding to seek his fortune in the West. He joined the Illinois State Geological Survey, which led to being elected surveyor of Rock County. After being admitted to the bar in 1842 he moved to Mineral Point, Wisconsin, and opened a bank. True to his Maine heritage and the influence of his brother William, he began buying timberland in Wisconsin and eastern Minnesota, making a fortune as a landowner.

Washburn's forays into Minnesota took him to the falls of St. Anthony. For no apparent reason except that he sensed an opportunity—he had no experience in flour milling—he formed the Minneapolis Mill Company and took control of waterpower on the west side of the falls. Two years later he partnered with Franklin Steele to build a dam across the Mississippi at the falls of St. Anthony, but he would wait another eight years to build his first mill. Public and military service delayed Washburn's plans. From 1855 to 1861 he served as a representative of Wisconsin to the U.S. Congress. At the onset of the Civil War he raised a regiment and became a colonel, even though he had no military training or experience. When the war ended, he resigned with the rank of major general. Before returning to Congress in 1867, followed by a stint as Wisconsin's governor in 1872, he built his first flour mill for a company that would eventually become General Mills.

Washburn, like Weyerhaeuser, thought big. Betting on the future of flour in Minnesota, he erected the first Washburn flour mill at a cost of $100,000. The mill could produce such large amounts of flour each day that most people expected it to be an expensive white elephant, which was why they labeled it "Washburn's Folly." Sure enough, two years later the mill failed under the management of two men who had leased it from Washburn. Undeterred, Washburn formed a new partnership with George Christian, an innovative thinker considered the best milling operator in the state. Like other successful entrepreneurs who lacked expertise in their chosen fields,

Cadwallader Washburn. Photograph courtesy of the Minnesota Historical Society.

Washburn built his empire by running the business and trusting others to manage the day-to-day operations.

Washburn and Christian faced an extremely competitive environment. By the end of the 1860s Minnesota had more than five hundred flour mills, including thirteen clustered around the falls of St. Anthony. The smaller mills ground flour in return for a share of the product. Washburn thought bigger.

Flour milling consisted of three steps: (1) separating the wheat from the chaff; (2) grinding the wheat between a pair of millstones; and (3) bolting, or sifting, the ground wheat through a fine cloth to separate the flour from the bran coating, or husks. The spring wheat grown by Minnesota farmers did not suit the milling process.

The Minneapolis milling district in 1905. Photograph by Charles J. Hibbard. Courtesy of the Minnesota Historical Society.

Its brittle husks crumbled into pieces that slipped through the bolting to discolor the flour. Crushing the kernel's oily germ diminished the flour's color, baking quality, and storage life, while the gluten was frequently sifted away, leaving less nutritious flour. To compete in national and international markets, Washburn and Christian had to find a way to make the flour from spring wheat competitive with the whiter and stronger flour made from winter wheat.

In 1868, Alexander Faribault brought a young French engineer to his mill in Faribault, Minnesota, to develop a purifier for spring wheat. Edmund La Croix, who had been using purifiers in France for several years, assembled one for the mill. George Christian heard about La Croix and hired him to install a purifier in the Washburn mill. After months of working in secret, La Croix deployed his new device in the spring of 1871. The purifier, which used air blasts to separate the husks from the rest of the wheat, made it possible for the Washburn mill to mass-produce white flour from spring wheat that was more nutritious than winter wheat while producing 12 percent more bread.

Demand—and profits—soared. La Croix left Washburn to install a purifier for a rival miller. Charles Pillsbury hired a Washburn miller familiar with the process to set up purifiers in his mills. The proliferation of the new process helped flour milling become Minnesota's first international business.

Washburn built a second, larger mill in 1874. He continued to add managerial talent to his company by partnering with Minneapolis lawyer John Crosby and hiring former mill owner William Dunwoody. Minneapolis millers entered the export market in 1877 when Dunwoody persuaded a Liverpool, England, company to place an order. Within three years flour exports from Minneapolis exceeded one million barrels.

It wasn't always a smooth road. On May 2, 1878, shortly after 6:00 P.M., a spark in Washburn's second mill ignited flour dust, causing an explosion that blew the roof hundreds of feet into the air. The blast ignited explosions in three nearby mills, and by morning three more mills had been wrecked and eighteen men killed. Nearly half the city's milling capacity had been destroyed.

Washburn learned of the disaster at the governor's residence in Madison. The next morning, he fulfilled a meeting obligation before boarding a train for Minneapolis. Two hours after arriving, amid smoldering debris, the sixty-year-old leader paced off dimensions for a newer, better mill. This time he installed dust-collecting machines to minimize the fire danger. Within a year he had completely restored capacity while adding a third mill, and within two years production had doubled.

While no entrepreneur could anticipate such a tragic event, few of the entrepreneurs profiled in this book have grown their companies without overcoming one or

Ruins of the Washburn "A" mill after the explosion in 1878. Photograph courtesy of the Minnesota Historical Society.

more serious, unexpected obstacles. Washburn did not allow the disaster to threaten his company. He did not hesitate to rebuild and expand, changing its name to Washburn, Crosby, and Company in 1879. When Washburn-Crosby flour won the gold medal for spring wheat at the Millers' International Exhibition in Cincinnati in 1880 (the genesis of Gold Medal brand flour), Cadwallader Washburn had to believe that his bet on the future had paid off.

Like his peers in this book, he didn't rest on his achievements. Washburn immediately tackled a second quality problem: as the sandstone millstones wore down, they mixed fine grit with the flour. Washburn and partner John Crosby learned that Hungarian millers were using rollers to grind wheat. In an early example of benchmarking best practices, they sent a man to Budapest to learn how the rollers worked, but the Hungarian mill owners wouldn't let him in the door. To get what he needed, he made a deal with one miller to study a roller system over several nights. He took the trade secrets back to Washburn-Crosby and helped equip one of its mills with steel rollers. The new rollers made better flour in greater amounts at lower costs.

As the size of flour mills grew and the technology improved, smaller mills found they could neither afford the financial investment nor retain their best managers. Seventeen firms operated twenty Minneapolis mills in 1876. By 1880, four companies, one of which was Washburn-Crosby, controlled nearly 90 percent of the city's milling capacity.

Cadwallader Washburn died in 1882 several months after suffering a stroke. Acknowledging his contributions to the flour-milling industry, an obituary noted, "He found milling a trade and left it a science."

Charles Pillsbury, one of Washburn's chief competitors and his equal as an entrepreneur, anticipated the transformation of his industry from many small companies to a few large ones. "The business of making flour had been brought to so close a point of competition that it is only possible to succeed by using the latest machinery and adopting the best system," Pillsbury observed. "It is purely a matter of business and must be

Gold Medal Flour billboard around 1915. Photograph courtesy of the Minnesota Historical Society.

conducted scientifically." His recognition of this major shift in his industry marks a critical point many entrepreneurs confront, when the rush to carve out new territory gives way to the grind of consolidating one of very few leadership positions. Often, this consolidation requires vision and courage as manageable budgets give way to major debt and obvious opportunities succumb to complex possibilities. It is at this point that those who build enduring enterprises assume the risks that can lead to greatness.

Pillsbury was an early adapter of the purifier invented by La Croix and one of the first to replace millstones with rollers. In 1879 he built the largest flour mill in the world, a distinction the mill held for decades. By 1889, C. A. Pillsbury and Company had surpassed Washburn-Crosby as the largest miller in Minneapolis.

Like Washburn, Charles Pillsbury had no flour-milling experience when he and his father bought part interest in a small, unprofitable Minneapolis mill shortly after arriving in Minnesota in 1869. Unlike Washburn, Pillsbury had an influential ally in the city: his uncle, John Pillsbury, was one of the city's most prominent citizens, an exceptional entrepreneur in his own right who owned and was involved in several businesses, invested in timberlands and real estate, and directed railroads, banks, and other businesses. He was the first three-term governor of Minnesota and is considered the "Father of the University of Minnesota."

Charles Alfred Pillsbury. Photograph from *The Northwestern Miller.* Courtesy of the Minnesota Historical Society.

Charles Pillsbury applied a similar diversity of skills to a single business. Shortly after installing purifiers in his mills, he came up with a marketing strategy to promote the superior quality of his flour. He labeled it Pillsbury's Best and began using an "XXXX" mark on all containers. The mark symbolized the best flour, a nod to the Middle Ages when bakers had marked the flour to be used in communion bread with three crosses.

Pillsbury used four X's to market his best flour. Photograph courtesy of the Minnesota Historical Society.

In 1882, to ensure a steady supply of wheat for his mills, Pillsbury started buying grain elevators along the Great Northern Railway in Minnesota and North Dakota. His company eventually owned and operated eighty elevators and warehouses. A year later he and his partners established one of the country's first employee profit-sharing plans. More than a decade later, Pillsbury was the first company to offer a packaged breakfast food, called Vitos, followed by packaged oatmeal under the name Flaked Oat Food.

Charles Pillsbury's broad view of the key qualities of a successful flour-milling company spurred innovations in technology, marketing, supply-chain management, employee involvement, and product. Although rarely first with original innovations, he quickly adopted new ideas that would improve his business. He had an unusual ability to understand the dynamics of his business, from the impact of farmers and grain merchants to the revolutionary improvements in flour milling, to the demands of customers. In 1897, two years before his death at age fifty-seven, he wrote, "Whatever else can be said about our business, one thing is sure, and that is that we have maintained the high standard of our flour, and have retained the confidence of all our customers."

By the time Washburn built his first mill, nearly every farmer in the young state grew wheat as his main crop. As the flour-milling industry flourished, two glaring needs created an extraordinary opportunity: the millers depended upon a ready and rapidly expanding supply of wheat to make flour, and Minnesota farmers had to get their large surpluses of wheat to the millers. Washburn and Pillsbury led the formation of a buyers cartel of Minneapolis millers to direct the wheat stored in elevators along the railroads to their mills instead of north to Duluth and east to Green Bay and Milwaukee, Wisconsin, but gaps in securing grain remained. With ample suppliers on one end of a railroad pipeline that fed the flour millers, the extraordinary opportunity to collect and ship the grain materialized.

Frank Peavey, Will Cargill, and John MacMillan

Shortly after arriving in Chicago in 1865 to seek his fortune, Frank Peavey got a job as a messenger and clerk for a grain firm. He was fifteen years old. A brief stint as a bank bookkeeper led to a bookkeeping job in Sioux City, Iowa.

Peavey believed that farming would inevitably become the backbone of the undeveloped West. His certainty convinced two local men to join him in a partnership to sell farm implements. It was a testament to Peavey's power of persuasion that his new partners trusted the opinion of an eighteen-year-old despite none of them knowing anything about farm implements. A year later the business burned to the ground, leaving the uninsured Peavey $1,800 in debt. He opened another farm-implements store, paid off his debts, and never again left a business unprotected.

As he talked with his customers, Peavey realized that many farmers were raising just enough grain to meet their own needs. Lacking a permanent market for their crops, they saw no reason to invest time and money to create a surplus. However, some surplus inevitably resulted, and Peavey started buying this excess grain. Needing a place to store it, he built a grain elevator in Sioux City in 1874, adding grain warehouses along the Dakota Southern Railway from Sioux City to Yankton, South Dakota.

Frank Peavey. Photograph courtesy of ConAgra Foods.

His next task was to secure the market that had eluded farmers. He traveled to Minneapolis to convince flour millers such as Washburn and Pillsbury that his system of collecting grain would provide them with the steady supply they needed. Many signed contracts on the spot, with Washburn's Minneapolis Millers Association becoming the Peavey Elevator Company's principal buyer. In 1875 the railway lines connecting Sioux City and St. Paul were consolidated to link Minneapolis–St. Paul, Omaha, and Chicago. Peavey persuaded railroad officials to let him add grain elevators throughout the system.

He moved his headquarters to Minneapolis in 1885 to be closer to his customers. The next year, he built the Midwest's largest elevator. Although a fire destroyed it a year later, Peavey, who had learned his lesson when he lost his first farm-implement business, had the elevator insured and built a new, larger one.

The fires and explosions that seemed to be an unavoidable product of grain storage drove insurance prices high, motivating Peavey to research the use of concrete grain tanks in place of flammable wood. He spent three years studying the possibility in Europe and the United States before sharing his thoughts with a Minneapolis contractor and builder. In addition to the problems inherent in an untested design, Peavey's peers all believed that wood was the only material suitable for storing grain because it would give when the grain was taken out. Peavey thought they were wrong, and in 1899 built an eighty-foot experimental grain silo out of concrete. Not only was the structural material untested, the construction process had never been used before. The contractor applied a "slip-form" technique, in which forms were filled with wet concrete and then moved up after it dried, resting on the lower, hardened walls. Hundreds of spectators turned out to watch "Peavey's Folly" collapse the first time the grain was removed, but the elevator worked flawlessly.

When Frank Peavey died two years later at the age of fifty-one, he had four of the largest steamships on the Great Lakes and broad investments in railroads, banks, and land. His greatest accomplishments in grain storage earned him the title of "Grain Elevator King of the World."

Throughout his career Peavey retained his entrepreneurial spirit, staying close to his customers, pursuing innovation, promoting growth, and anticipating change. Just as he had recognized the enormous opportunity in helping farmers find a market for their grain, he remained alert to new needs and challenges as his industry matured. In a speech shortly before his death, he said, "Our field is larger, our opportunities greater and our competition keener. And to be successful we must change with conditions and accept them as they exist today."

Will Cargill reveled in change. Like Frank Peavey, he followed the railroads to build his grain-elevator empire. In fact, in 1895, Peavey, Cargill, and another company owned almost all the grain-storage capacity in the strategically located port of Duluth. The scope of the Cargill enterprise, however, eventually outgrew Peavey's business. For the most part, Peavey worked alone, while Cargill built his empire with the help of two brothers and his son-in-law, John MacMillan. While Peavey applied his entrepreneur-

The "slip-form" concrete elevator Peavey built in 1899. Photograph courtesy of the Minnesota Historical Society.

ial skills only to his grain storage and distribution business, Cargill tried prospecting for coal, running flour mills, mining for silver and copper, building railroads, buying timberland, and developing land. Both men took full advantage of the farmers' need to market their grain, but Cargill did not stop there, dabbling in any number of interests that would eventually help shape the W. W. Cargill Company of today.

Like Peavey, Washburn, Pillsbury, and others, Will Cargill went west to seek his fortune, but his journey stopped at the end of the McGregor Western railroad line in northeastern Iowa. A twenty-one-year-old farm boy fresh from Civil War service, Cargill found a partner and opened a grain warehouse. As the railroad laid track north, Cargill moved with it, adding warehouses in Cresco and Lime Springs on the Minnesota border. In 1867 two of his brothers joined him. They saved money by living in one of the warehouses, sleeping on cots in the same room they used as an office and cooking on a potbellied stove.

When the McGregor Western met the Minnesota Central railroad in Austin, Will Cargill built a warehouse in Austin. When the Southern Minnesota railroad connected Austin to Albert Lea, he moved to Albert Lea and erected another warehouse. He continued to buy land and build warehouses along the Southern Minnesota line, increasing his storage capacity by 400 percent despite a financial panic and a natural disaster.

The panic of 1873 caused the failure of many country grain elevators. In the same

Will Cargill. Photograph courtesy of Cargill, Inc.

year a plague of Rocky Mountain locusts descended on Minnesota, feasting on what-ever farmers were growing but showing a preference for wheat. The following spring the grasshoppers' eggs hatched and the pestilence magnified. With little formal relief available, farm families lost everything. The infestation lasted five summers until a storm, or the need for a fresh food supply, freed Minnesota of the insects. (Another theory concerning their departure gave credit to Governor John Pillsbury, who de-livered a "Grasshopper Message" to the state legislature in 1877, calling for a day of prayer, fasting, and humiliation. That summer the locusts left and Minnesota farmers reaped a bountiful wheat harvest.)

Will Cargill weathered both storms in the same way investors make money in bear markets: He confidently bought cheap grain elevators and warehouses and waited for the natural and financial difficulties to run their course. By 1875 he and a partner owned forty-seven warehouses in twenty-seven locations and his net worth was esti-mated at $50,000.

In 1874 he had moved his headquarters and his family to La Crosse, Wisconsin, where he built an elegant house across the street from the equally elegant home of Duncan MacMillan. He began integrating his small country elevators and his coal inter-ests through the railroad, collecting and hauling grain east to Chicago and Milwaukee and coal west to La Crosse, where he sold it to farmers through his own retail store.

The move to La Crosse was also significant because the intersection of the Cargill and MacMillan families made an enduring Cargill enterprise possible. Both had ex-perience as grain merchants. Both pursued financial opportunities in several areas. Yet the business approaches of the company's first two leaders, Will Cargill and his suc-cessor and son-in-law, John MacMillan, provided very different strengths when the growing company needed them most.

Cargill's desire to pursue any opportunity that presented itself reflected an energet-ic yet often undisciplined approach. When he died in 1909 at the age of sixty-four, he left no will and a trail of debts, many unrecorded and not evident until the creditors began demanding payment. Most of the assets of the W. W. Cargill Company had to be liquidated to pay these debts, but John MacMillan was able to keep the Cargill Ele-vator Company in Minneapolis intact.

MacMillan had been prepared for this new challenge by early adversity in his own career. In 1891, at the age of twenty-two, he and his two younger brothers went to Fort Worth, Texas, to start a business trading wheat. Like Cargill and Peavey, they built grain elevators along the Fort Worth and Denver City railroad. Coincidentally, panic and pestilence plagued the MacMillan brothers as well.

The panic of 1893 finished the railroad, grasshoppers descended, and a drought hit, and the MacMillans held on for five difficult years. At one point Will Cargill discussed a job in Green Bay, Wisconsin, for his son-in-law, but John MacMillan, in true entrepreneurial spirit, chafed at the thought. "I don't think there is anything degrading in working for another," he wrote to his wife. "What hurt was the idea of

John MacMillan. Photograph courtesy of Cargill, Inc.

failure—failure to make a success of what I managed and the idea that would almost necessarily follow, that I was unworthy of the position I had occupied and that henceforth I would find my level in carrying out what others directed instead of others carrying out what I directed."

Assessing his situation, MacMillan recognized the positive lessons in his hard-earned experience. "I am conscious of or at least have a feeling that I have financial and business ability," he wrote. "My character is broadening and hardening under such a stress of experience. My judgment is growing keener and my powers of observation and reason stronger and the day will yet come when all I have suffered will prove a powerful lever to aid in ultimate success."

After his Texas operation closed in 1896, MacMillan ran an Arkansas lumber operation for Cargill before moving to Minneapolis to take over the grain business in 1903. His day had come. His experiences had shaped a conservative approach that avoided the cyclical swings of the grain business, but they had also given him a keen sense for business opportunities and a strategic view of the entire organization. He understood how traders think, but he also understood the need to base decisions on facts and he demanded those facts promptly and accurately. Over the next thirty years, John MacMillan transformed Cargill from a scattered collection of businesses into a multi-faceted organization guided by a strong sense of purpose.

The Cargills and MacMillans illustrate a common phenomenon that continues to hold true today: involving family in the creation of an enduring enterprise. One of the best-known sibling endeavors of this period, which will be described later in this chapter, involved the Merritt brothers, widely known as the "seven iron men." While brotherly arrangements flourished, a more common partnership in the late 1800s involved fathers and sons, such as those who built Mayo Clinic and the H. B. Fuller Company.

Cargill built elevators along railroad lines throughout the Upper Midwest. Photograph courtesy of Cargill, Inc.

W. W. Mayo, William Mayo, and Charles Mayo

Although Mayo Clinic traces its heritage to the frontier practice of William Worrall
Mayo, it owes its transformation into a world-class clinic to his sons, William and
Charles, who grew up helping their father and knowing that they too would become
physicians. The unique characteristics of Mayo Clinic—a passion for improving medicine, a reliance on interlocking talents, an eagerness to share information—started
with W. W. Mayo and his attitude toward his sons and his profession. A doctor who
emigrated from England to the United States in 1846, Mayo established a practice in
1864 in Rochester, Minnesota, a town southeast of the capital city, to examine new
recruits for the Union Army. He frequently involved his young sons in his work, from
cleaning and caring for his equipment to observing and helping with patients. In 1883
his oldest son, William, finished medical school and joined his practice. That year a
tornado devastated north Rochester.

As it had for other entrepreneurs, tragedy spun the Mayo practice into a new
orbit. In an effort to care for those injured by the tornado, W. W. Mayo asked Mother
Alfred Moes, founder of the Sisters of St. Francis, to allow him to move them into the
convent. She agreed. While the health of those hurt in the storm improved, Mother
Alfred recognized the ongoing need for a local hospital. She proposed the construction of a new hospital, built and staffed by the sisters, to W. W. Mayo, with the condition that he would provide its medical care. He doubted that such a venture would
succeed in a small town, but Mother Alfred persisted, promising that her order of

William Warrall Mayo with sons Charles (left) and William. Photograph by Clarence G. Stearns.
Courtesy of the Minnesota Historical Society.

Charles Mayo captivated his audience during surgery at Mayo Clinic in 1913. Photograph courtesy of the Minnesota Historical Society.

sisters would raise $40,000 to build the facility. Saint Marys Hospital opened in 1889, and it has continued to grow alongside Mayo Clinic.

Charles Mayo joined the practice of his father and brother in 1888, and a few years later, as the clinic expanded, the Mayos added their first partner to the family practice. In 1901 Henry Plummer joined "the Mayos' clinic." He developed the systems that allowed the group practice to flourish, from designing a common medical record to creating lifts and conveyors for moving records and x-rays, to installing one of the world's first telephone paging systems. These systems, combined with the inquisitive and collaborative spirit of W. W. Mayo and the medical genius of his sons, laid the foundation for what has become an internationally known medical center. It is a tribute to the Mayos' foresight that their organization thrived after the deaths of W. W. Mayo in 1911 and William and Charles Mayo in 1939.

Like most successful entrepreneurial families, the Mayo sons shared their father's passion. Their father, in turn, recognized his sons' ability to build upon what he had started. Such a transition trips up many promising young companies. A brilliant entrepreneur survives hard times and relishes prosperity in part because he or she feels in control of every decision. The founder chooses the course, decides every matter, bears all hardship, worries about every threat, and acts daily upon his or her dream. When self-reliance must give way to dependence on others, depending on family is often the only way a hard-driving entrepreneur can keep the business going. Even then, the family member's dreams and talents must support the transition, as Harvey Fuller discovered.

Harvey Fuller

Harvey Fuller was the first paste manufacturer in Minnesota. He had come from Chicago in 1887 because he liked the entrepreneurial spirit of St. Paul and appreciated the ready supply of flour. He spent hours at an iron kettle on the family's wood-burning stove, seeking a combination of flour, water, and chemicals that would produce the best wallpaper paste. He incorporated his Fuller Manufacturing Company that same year with $600 in capital.

Like many entrepreneurs, Fuller ran his entire operation alone. He was the chemist, paste maker, packager, deliveryman, and bookkeeper. To help pay the bills, he supplied ink to the city's schools, bottled laundry blueing, and mixed paste for paperhangers and industrial customers. When the Fuller Manufacturing Company was only a year old, however, Fuller's oldest son, sixteen-year-old Albert, started working for him. Albert immediately took on some of his father's responsibilities, including conducting his own experiments on a new mucilage formula. In 1893 father and son came up with a drywall cleaner. Other new products followed, yet despite their successes Albert had his own entrepreneurial dreams, and he eventually moved to another part of the country to pursue them.

The company declined until shortly after World War I, when Harvey Fuller Jr. took over as president. While he did not have the innovative skills of his father and

H. B. Fuller and family in 1895, when Albert (standing, right) helped his father develop new products. Harvey (seated, right) helped his father's company recover after World War I. Photograph courtesy of the H. B. Fuller Company.

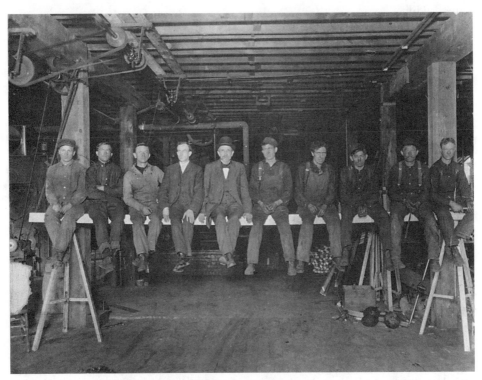

A prolific inventor, H. B. Fuller developed this scaffolding system in the early 1900s. He is seated in the middle, wearing a bow tie. Photograph courtesy of the H. B. Fuller Company.

A label from a box of Fuller White Pearl Dry Paste. Photograph courtesy of the H. B. Fuller Company.

brother, he added something even more valuable at the time: the ability to lead and grow a company. One of his first acts was to hire a chemist to develop industrial adhesives, primarily for affixing labels to cans. The new line of adhesives saved the company and established H. B. Fuller as an enduring enterprise.

In some cases, the entrepreneur who starts an enterprise is able to establish it so soundly that his children inherit a growing, profitable business. Such was the case with James J. Hill.

James J. Hill

Railroad baron James Hill did not follow in his father's footsteps, but that did not prevent him from imagining the day when he would make a significant mark on the world. That rare belief is evident in the fact that, as a thirteen-year-old boy, James Hill decided to take the middle name Jerome after the brother of emperor Napoleon Bonaparte.

Adversity in his childhood did not diminish his expectations. When he was a boy, James Hill was shooting arrows when he pulled back on the bowstring and the bow snapped, sending the arrow into his right eye. A doctor returned the eyeball to its socket and restored muscular control, but the optic nerve was destroyed and he was blind in that eye. The accident had no effect on his entrepreneurial career, although it did prevent him from fighting in the Civil War.

While growing up in Rockwood, Ontario, Hill was exposed to stories of Napoleon and other historical figures through a brilliant teacher. In addition to giving him a sense of history, the teacher, who had Hill as a student for four years until he left school at age fourteen, taught him how to understand mathematics, write legibly, and communicate clearly. That few young men of that time possessed such knowledge and skills was evident when the eighteen-year-old Hill arrived in St. Paul in 1856: He

James Jerome Hill. Photograph by Ludovici's Photographic and Crayon Studios. Courtesy of the Minnesota Historical Society.

stepped off the steamboat ready to start a job he had been offered during the ride. Brunson, Lewis & White, the agents for the steamboat company, were so impressed with his abilities they had hired him on the spot.

Although Hill worked with steamboats, his first love was the railroad. He spent his first ten years in St. Paul working for steamboat and railroad companies, during which time he learned the fundamentals and secrets of river and railroad transportation, whole-sale merchandising, commodity trading, and logistics. During the Civil War he learned to buy and sell goods at a profit and move products in the least expensive ways. He used this new knowledge to become an expert in his adopted industry. Hill observed where immigrants were settling and anticipated their transportation needs. He recognized how farmers needed the railroads to move their grain and how railroads needed farmers as customers. Like W. W. Cargill and Frank Peavey, he saw the railroad as a lifeline to new frontiers, a conduit through which goods and money and the people who needed them flowed, and through which the flour millers of Minneapolis could get the wheat they required.

It's not surprising then that Hill's first venture involved the railroad. With two partners, each of whom invested $5,000, he used his savings of $2,500 to start a company that transferred freight from steamboats to the St. Paul and Pacific Railroad. It was not an instant success. Although he had exclusive rights for the freight transfer, his company's income in 1866, its first year, was just $2,000.

About the same time, he worked out an agreement with St. Anthony flour millers to store their flour in his warehouse over the winter. His contract with the railroad meant the millers' flour would be the first shipped in the spring, which helped Hill lock up their business. To get the most out of his warehouse, he bought large quantities of wood in the summer for sale to homeowners and the railroad in the winter.

He didn't stop there. Hill believed that coal was a better fuel than wood for railroads. He struck a deal to buy Pennsylvania coal, then convinced the St. Paul and Pacific to use coal in its shops and forges. His coal business quintupled from 1870 to 1874.

As it did with Will Cargill, the panic of 1873 helped Hill when railroads realized that their fixed costs stayed the same no matter how much they carried, which meant they needed to carry as much as possible. Hill understood their dilemma and negotiated low rates to carry large amounts of his coal.

While these enterprises kept Hill busy, he had his eyes on a much larger opportunity. As a student of the railroads, he watched the flow of immigrants to the Red River Valley in west-central Minnesota and saw their need to get their crops to market. He understood that the railroad was easily the cheapest form of land transportation, and that a railroad into the valley would cut almost an entire year off the time it took farmers to market their crops. He had followed the struggles of the St. Paul and Pacific since 1865, when its Dutch owners started pouring what ended up being $13 million into the railroad. Northern Pacific took over the railroad in 1870, but its leaders, who were focused on building a railroad from Wisconsin's Green Bay to Washington's Puget Sound, failed to recognize the value of connecting to St. Paul.

As the Northern Pacific stumbled, Hill gathered information about the railroad and the market. Like few others, he understood how a railroad could be profitable, that the winner in a competitive field was often not only able to do business at the lowest cost, but willing to outlast the competition to stay ahead.

In February 1877 he learned it would cost approximately $5.5 million to buy the St. Paul and Pacific. Based on his extensive research, Hill estimated that the railroad's track was worth $11.4 million and its equipment worth $800,000; it had surplus property worth $400,000 that could be sold off; it had town sites on its main land worth

The St. Paul and Pacific Railway station at Washington Avenue and Third Avenue North in Minneapolis, 1874. Photograph courtesy of the Minnesota Historical Society.

$200,000; and it had a land grant of 2,643,000 acres lying, for the most part, in well-settled areas conservatively worth $6.7 million. For an investment of $5.5 million, Hill and his partners bought a railroad worth nearly $20 million. He signed the deal in the fall of 1877, risking everything he had, in the fourth year of a great depression, on the soundness of his judgment.

And then he went to work. He connected the Red River Valley with Winnipeg, Manitoba, and received two million acres of land for completing the rail line on time. Two seasons of bumper crops followed. Net earnings for Hill's railroad surpassed $1 million in 1879. Next, he aimed his railroad at Puget Sound, a notion that, true to the conventional wisdom of the day, became known as "Hill's Folly." A hands-on leader like Weyerhaeuser, he studied the land his track would travel and planned exactly where it would go. He analyzed all grades and curves himself. He insisted on using the best materials. Most of all, he understood that a railroad was never really finished. Success came to those who never stood still.

Unlike other railroad barons who built their railroads around a population, Hill built a population around his railroad. He sent agents to Europe to show potential immigrants the agricultural possibilities in the Northwest. He encouraged settlement along his routes by letting immigrants ride the train for $10. He even imported cattle and gave them to farmers free of charge if they worked land near his railroads. As a result of his promotional efforts, more than six million acres of Montana land were settled in two years.

Hill and the golden spike signifying the completion of his railroad from St. Paul to Puget Sound, 1893. Photograph courtesy of the Minnesota Historical Society.

Hill's railroad reached Puget Sound, a little more than eighteen hundred miles from St. Paul, in 1893. The city of St. Paul proposed a grand celebration to honor his achievement, but he suggested the city use the celebration funds to build a new library, offering to match whatever the city raised. The panic of 1893 stalled the project until 1913, when work finally began on two adjoining libraries, the St. Paul Public Library and the James J. Hill Library. The endowment Hill left still funds the Hill library.

In 1907, at the age of sixty-nine, he turned over leadership of the Great Northern Railway to his son, Louis. In the fifty-one years since James J. Hill first arrived in St. Paul, the territory with a few thousand inhabitants had become a state teeming with a million Minnesotans.

Hill never lost his love of railroading. In 1912, four years before he died, he said, "Most men who have really lived have had, in some shape, their great adventure. The railway is mine." James J. Hill lived the adventure. When he first visited the Red River Valley in 1870 and imagined the possibilities of its future transportation needs, he traveled as an explorer, by stagecoach and dogsled. He made tea with snow and slept on the ground. Despite the primitive conditions, Hill envisioned an opportunity others had missed. In less than a decade, he would own his own railroad and link the valley to the Canadian Pacific railroad and Winnipeg. By the turn of the century his domain stretched to the Pacific, earning him the well-deserved title—a title he had foreshadowed as a boy—of "Empire Builder."

Leonidas Merritt

As with James J. Hill, the roots of the Merritts' future sprouted when the family's sons, led by Leonidas, or Lon, as he was known, were boys. "Soon after we moved West," Lon later recalled, "my father made a trip into the woods beyond Duluth. When he came back he told us he thought there might be ore on the Missabe. He threw out the suggestion that if any of us boys were ever up that way it might pay us to look around and see what we could find. That remark stuck in my crop."

Missabe, or Mesabi, is a Chippewa word that means "a giant buried in the hills." For years the ore in Minnesota's Mesabi Iron Range was a sleeping giant hidden to iron hunters who could not see past their own experience. Miners expected to find vertical deposits of hard ore. They could not conceive of the possibility of soft iron ore just below the surface.

The Merritts weren't burdened by such ingrained biases. They worked on railroad survey crews, engaged in trade along the coast of Lake Superior, built the first sailing vessel at the head of the lake, and bought timberlands. They were explorers, discoverers, developers, and entrepreneurs, but they were not miners.

In fact, for fifteen years expert geologists and miners told them that no iron ore deposits of much value would be found on the Mesabi Range. The Merritts kept looking, led by the confident and untiring Lon. While they walked the forests to assess the quantity and quality of the timber, they looked for any signs of ore deposits. During one such foray, Cassius Merritt was scanning the pine to assess its value when he

The Merritt family. Leonidas is standing, left, with his hand on the shoulder of Cassius. Photograph courtesy of the Minnesota Historical Society.

tripped over a rock and fell. Dusting himself off, he picked up the rock and wondered if it might be iron ore. An assayer informed him that it was high-grade Bessemer ore, a discovery that prompted extensive surveys of the area.

Lon Merritt arranged for the mapping of the entire Mesabi region, sending crews to conduct test drillings. They found nothing. As their capital dwindled, he and one of his brothers returned to Duluth to seek new funding. On November 16, 1890, the wheels of a heavy test-pit crew wagon burrowed into the soft soil a few miles east of Virginia, Minnesota, to reveal a red, powdery substance. The head of the crew collected fifty pounds of the red earth and brought it to Duluth to be assayed. It was 64 percent iron. Two members of the Merritt family wrote about the impact of that event: "To all of us, it was a day of days, but to Lon, the natural leader . . . whose goodly fortune had been spent in this determined and hectic search for iron, to Lon, whose vision had by turn swept and driven us all along toward this hour, what it must have meant in the secret places of his generous heart!" Lon seized the moment. He immediately expanded the Merritts' land holding in the Mesabi Iron Range, leasing 141 quarter-sections from the state for fifty years for just $100 apiece. Over the next two years, an estimated fifteen thousand prospectors invaded the range. Some, like Frank Hibbing, struck it rich. The great majority found nothing.

Being first amid the crush of prospectors motivated the cash-strapped Merritts to seek urgent solutions to three huge obstacles, the first of which was finding a market for the ore. While the country needed iron and steel, steel-plant operators were skeptical about the value of this soft ore. Once its utility was proven, however, the involvement of John D. Rockefeller, Andrew Carnegie, and J. P. Morgan in the Iron Range, and the eventual formation of the U.S. Steel Corporation that resulted, created a market that would purchase 43 million tons of Minnesota ore by 1900 and 208.6 million tons from 1901 to 1910.

The second problem was getting the ore to market. From their experience as lumbermen, the Merritts knew how difficult it was to move heavy goods long distances. To get their ore to Duluth, they had to build a railroad from the Iron Range, docks in Duluth, and barges to carry the ore to the steel plants in Ohio and Pennsylvania.

In October 1892 the railroad built by the Merritts connected to the Duluth and Winnipeg railroad twenty-five miles west of Duluth. In return for guaranteed ore shipments, the Duluth and Winnipeg had agreed to provide a large number of ore cars. The railroad reneged on its end of the deal, so the Merritts decided to build their own ore cars and extend their railroad all the way to Duluth.

Their third problem, financing their venture, threatened the enterprise. Undercapitalized from the start, the Merritts were more than $2 million in debt late in 1892 when Lon pushed ahead with plans to build ore cars and add onto the railroad. Their frenzy to quickly put every piece into place left them overextended when the panic of 1893 hit. To pay their bills, the Merritts put stock in their railroad on the market. Rockefeller bought a half-million dollars' worth. Sensing the Merritts' precarious position, a buyer offered them $8 million for their business. They declined.

The Merritts' first mine near Mountain Iron, Minnesota, 1892. Photograph courtesy of the Minnesota Historical Society.

When they fell behind again, they approached Rockefeller through agents about a loan, which he made with the stipulation that the Merritts would assume interest in his mining ventures while he got control of their Mesabi properties. The consolidated stock failed to hold its value and the Merritts had to sell ninety thousand shares in their Mountain Iron Company to Rockefeller in January 1894 for $10 a share. Their shooting star had burned itself out.

Their agreement included a stipulation that the Merritts could redeem fifty-five thousand shares in one year, with interest. The shares roughly equaled the amount they owed Rockefeller. Only one of the Merritts redeemed his stock. The others eventually took Rockefeller to court. The two parties settled out of court in 1897 for a reported $1 million, all of which went to the Merritts' creditors.

Few examples of the peril of being undercapitalized are more dramatic than the plight of the Merritts. Some could argue that they gambled big and lost, but their risks were no more outrageous than those of Weyerhaeuser, Washburn, Cargill, Peavey, and Hill, although the pace at which they moved was considerably faster. Others could argue that they entered an arena for which they were ill prepared, but again, the entrepreneurial peers of their day often lacked extensive knowledge of every area they pursued.

The difference between the Merritts and those who created enduring enterprises seems to come down to financial resources. Although Weyerhaeuser, Washburn, Cargill, Peavey, and Hill also started with little, they developed strong relationships with bankers and wealthy potential partners. While the Merritts tried to finance their operation alone, these other entrepreneurs secured sound financial backing. The Merritts rushed into a number of expensive ventures, while the others moved more slowly, waiting for one area to stabilize before moving on to another.

At the same time, the Merritts' fate turned on a national financial crisis they could not have predicted. That it happened when they were most vulnerable contributed as much as anything to the demise of their dreams. Although they were unable to claim credit for building an enduring enterprise, their determination to discover ore on the Iron Range was largely responsible for creating a new industry in Minnesota.

The influx of miners to the Mesabi Iron Range marked the last prolonged era of immigration to Minnesota. Each era formed to take advantage of Minnesota's greatest natural resources. Weyerhaeuser and the lumbermen came first from New England, France, Ireland, and Switzerland. Washburn, Pillsbury, Cargill, and Peavey served the farmers who arrived from Germany, Norway, Denmark, and Sweden. The Merritts and the mining industry drew eastern Europeans to the Iron Range. James J. Hill moved people and products where the needs and opportunities lay.

These exceptional entrepreneurs not only founded companies that helped make Minnesota the star of the north, they also created opportunities for others to pursue their business dreams. Alexander Hartman's Duluth Electric Company flourished when the Merritts discovered iron ore just two years after the company started, drawing thousands of new customers to the area. Fred Nash relied on James J. Hill's railroads to ship fresh food to small rural markets, establishing a warehousing and sales operation that became the Nash Finch Company. Jesse Northrup and Charles Braslan were seed experts who set up shop in Minneapolis in 1884 because they believed in the benefits of northern-grown seed and in the promise of an agricultural region prospering through the efforts of Hill, Washburn, Pillsbury, Peavey, and Cargill. Northrup survived a disastrous fire and bankruptcy to found Northrup King. And then there was Richard Hankinson.

Richard Hankinson

His friends called Richard Hankinson a dreamer, which must have made his job as superintendent of construction for Northwestern Telegraph in Minneapolis seem pretty mundane. When an associate told him about the possibilities of a new invention called the telephone, Hankinson took two home with him to try them out. He rigged up one in the den closet without telling anyone, then ran a line to the other in his telegraph office, where he shouted into the receiver. His wife heard the noise, traced it to the closet, opened the door, and gasped when her husband wasn't there.

Despite the prank, Hankinson persuaded his wife, who was one of the leading sopranos in Minneapolis, to help him promote the new device by singing church hymns over

Richard Hankinson. Photograph courtesy of the Minnesota Historical Society.

it. His first telephone exchange in city hall was made out of an old sewing-machine stand and had eleven telephones connected to it. That number would grow to seven hundred within two years. Hankinson's company was incorporated as Northwestern Telephone in 1878.

South Telephone Exchange for the Northwestern Bell Telephone Company, circa 1895. Photograph courtesy of the Minnesota Historical Society.

By the turn of the century, the drama of launching businesses that helped settle a frontier had been concluded. The entrepreneurs who would follow would more closely resemble Hankinson and Northrup than Hill and Weyerhaeuser, but although their areas of success would not achieve the scope of these early entrepreneurial giants, they would continue the tradition of building enduring enterprises that served essential needs.

Seizing Opportunity (1890–1915)

Theodore Hamm

In September 1894, in a newly constructed edifice decorated with banners and bunting, Theodore Hamm opened a modern brewery. He had been making beer for more than thirty years in the same small building on St. Paul's east side, a butcher turned brewer by circumstance more than intent.

Hamm and his wife, Louise, had moved to an area of St. Paul near Fort Snelling in 1856, where he raised and butchered cattle while she opened and operated a *Biergarten*. The fort provided a sense of security for the German immigrants whose meat and meals attracted other Germans to settle nearby. Despite the comfort of family and friends, however, Theodore Hamm longed for adventure. The second gold rush of 1861 promised instant riches to those bold enough to head west. Wild stories swept through the small community, and Hamm couldn't resist regaling his wife with tales of fortunes easily gained. Louise Hamm would have none of it. She persuaded her husband to stay home with her and their three children and leave prospecting to others.

Theodore Hamm did not give up easily. Learning that his best friend planned to join the rush, Hamm mortgaged his home and *Biergarten* and gave the money to his friend in exchange for a percentage of the riches he found and the rights to his friend's brewery if something went wrong—which it did: the friend died shortly after arriving in California. Hamm inherited a brewery about which he knew nothing, located on the east side of St. Paul, miles from the safety of the fort and the comfort of the small German community. The Hamms moved into living quarters attached to the brewery. When Theodore Hamm asked an old friend who was working at the Schlitz

Theodore and Louise Hamm and family, circa 1880. Photograph courtesy of the Minnesota Historical Society.

Brewery in Milwaukee to become Hamm's first brew master, Jacob Schmidt and his wife and children moved in with the Hamms.

Schmidt ran the brewery while Hamm returned to raising cattle, dressing meat for sale to the growing population of St. Paul, and operating a small mill that ground wheat and made malt for his brewery. When farmers showed up with grain to grind, he invited them to stay for beer and dinner. Soon Louise Hamm and Katherine Schmidt realized they were running a free restaurant, so they opened a new *Biergarten*.

The first brutal winter at the brewery isolated the families from many of their German friends. The next spring Hamm began selling nearby land to his laborers to encourage them to build homes on St. Paul's east side. His generous spirit pervaded the brewery, which had a policy of free beer for workers. Brewery veterans followed an unwritten rule: no overindulging. Workers who did were reprimanded the first time and fired the second. As Hamm's son, William, assumed more responsibilities at the growing brewery, he established a system of giving each employee six tickets every morning for six glasses of beer available at 10:00 A.M., noon, and 4:00 P.M.

Employees of Hamm's Brewery in the early 1880s. Photograph courtesy of the Minnesota Historical Society.

Theodore Hamm's employees were also his friends, and he wanted to make sure their interests were represented in decisions concerning the brewery. He encouraged them to form a union, and at their first meeting without him, the workers voted on a union president: Hamm. While the flustered owner appreciated their faith in him, he declined the position, pointing out that, since he was already making the decisions, they really needed to choose someone else to speak for their best interests.

Through Hamm's gentle leadership and Schmidt's brewing skills, the Theodore Hamm Brewing Company outgrew its original space, moving into a new building in 1894. The company was officially incorporated in 1896 with a capitalization of $3 million. Theodore Hamm died in 1903.

Theodore Hamm's success illustrates the opportunities for Minnesota entrepreneurs at the turn of the century. Businesses built upon the state's three greatest natural resources dominated Minnesota's economy, creating ample commercial possibilities for breweries, dairies, meatpacking plants, financial services, transportation services, utilities, retail stores, building materials, consumer goods, insurance, and other ventures. The nature of the enterprises that profited from the state's resources and the steady stream of immigrants they attracted inspired a diverse economy.

Minnesota became the third-ranking lumber state in 1900, the highest position it ever reached. Lumbermen worked fast because of a diminishing supply caused by fierce competition and fire: a disastrous forest fire destroyed the town of Hinckley in 1894 and another fire devastated Chisholm in 1908. It has been estimated that fire

Hamm's new brewery opened in 1894 in St. Paul. Photograph by Palmquist. Courtesy of the Minnesota Historical Society.

took more timber than lumbermen, a threat that motivated lumbermen to beat the fires by cutting faster.

Lumber production gradually declined until 1905 before dropping off rapidly. Sawmills started to close as the logging boom ran its course; Minnesota ceased to be a significant lumber state by the end of the 1920s.

Despite its relatively brief reign, lumbering fueled Minnesota's rapid early growth. It created thousands of jobs, from cutting timber to operating sawmills to constructing wood buildings. It infused the new state with the capital required to support flour milling, mining, and other promising industries. And it helped attract and train entrepreneurs who learned how lumber businesses worked and applied their knowledge to their own dreams. Two of the entrepreneurs featured in this chapter, George Draper Dayton and Hans Andersen, owned lumberyards before launching their own enduring enterprises.

In 1890 Minneapolis became the world's leading market for wheat. Flour milling remained the state's leading industry into the 1920s. The Twin Cities became a major financial center because flour millers needed large amounts of capital to keep them going while they bought wheat for cash, then waited until they could mill the wheat and sell the flour months later. For example, the first customers of investment bankers C. Palmer Jaffrey and Harry Piper included Washburn-Crosby and Pillsbury.

Flour milling also generated other food businesses, such as cereal manufacturing and breweries. Brewers, like early sawmill operators, flour millers, and meatpackers, served local markets and rarely competed against each other. Two technological innovations around the turn of the century, pasteurization of beer and refrigerated railroad cars, made it possible for brewers such as Theodore Hamm to offer their beer to broader markets.

Like the lumber industry, the flour-milling industry waned in Minnesota during the 1920s. Mills closed as companies built new operations in Kansas City, Missouri, and Buffalo, New York, as well as other cities offering better freight rates. The decline of flour milling hardly meant the end of agriculture as a commercial force in Minnesota, however. Farmers had long been moving away from wheat as their sole source of income, a trend that accelerated during the grasshopper plague of the mid-1870s. Since growing wheat year after year depleted the soil, farmers started small dairy operations and grew corn and oats, which they could now market through an expanding railroad network. Advances in machinery improved efficiency and production. Minnesota agriculture in general spawned a number of businesses such as Nash Finch, Northrup King, and the Minnesota Valley Canning Company (Green Giant), as well as a variety of industries including meatpacking, dairy, and bakery products. Four of the top five meatpackers eventually established plants in South St. Paul while the state's leading meatpacker, George Hormel, founded his company in Austin in 1891.

Iron-ore mining, which tapped into Minnesota's third great natural resource, propelled growth in population on the three ranges—Mesabi, Vermilion, and Cuyana—from twenty-five thousand in 1900 to one hundred thousand just twenty years later. While the number of miners varied from twenty thousand during boom times to four thousand during recessions, the area's population remained fairly stable. The next chapter will describe how one entrepreneur, Carl Wickman, took advantage of the miners' need for transportation to create an enduring enterprise.

In 1900 fewer than 5 percent of Minnesotans worked in manufacturing, which required little skill or advanced technology. Minnesota's manufacturing advantage lay in its ability to transform timber, wheat, and iron ore into essential products, but that advantage would weaken as resources dwindled and competition from other parts of the country increased. As a result, new entrepreneurs had to find innovative ways to identify unmet needs, add value to basic materials, and establish new industries.

Hans Andersen

In the summer of 1903, forty-nine-year-old Hans Andersen's experiences and circumstances aligned with an unmet business need and his own innovative thinking to help launch the window industry.

Andersen's experiences began as a solitary sixteen-year-old Danish immigrant landing in Portland, Maine. He planned on settling somewhere in the Midwest and began working his way across the country, choosing jobs where no one spoke Danish so he

Hans Andersen. Photograph courtesy of the Andersen Corporation.

would be forced to learn English. One of his early jobs involved working with teams of men to pry up tree stumps, where the first English words he learned were "All together, boys." The bond he felt for his fellow workers would continue to shape his business philosophy for the rest of his life.

Andersen chose to settle in Spring Valley, Minnesota, because few Scandinavians lived there and he could continue to improve his English. He ran a lumberyard until the market for lumber declined. The largest sawmill in nearby La Crosse, Wisconsin, hired him to sell a huge surplus of lumber. His success at the venture encouraged him to operate a sawmill of his own in St. Cloud, Minnesota. The mill prospered until it was destroyed by fire. He rebuilt, but the panic of 1893 dried up the market for lumber. In the winter of 1896 he heard about another opportunity to sell surplus lumber, this time in Hudson, Wisconsin. Unable to move lumber across the St. Croix River to the Twin Cities market, an owner eagerly sold his entire supply of one million board feet to Andersen, who solved the logistics problem by building a temporary pathway across the frozen river. He sold all the lumber.

Andersen stayed in Hudson to manage a sawmill, hiring experienced workers from his previous mill in St. Cloud to operate it. That fall, when the owners wanted to lay people off as business slowed, he refused and resigned, opening a lumberyard and offering his St. Cloud workers jobs. He had brought them from St. Cloud to Hudson and had no intention of abandoning them.

By 1903 Hans Andersen understood the lumber industry, from logging to milling to selling wood to customers. He had endured the cyclical nature of running a lumberyard and believed that adding value by manufacturing wood products would smooth earnings and improve profits. He had an idea for what he should manufacture, but first he needed to ascertain the intentions of two potential job candidates.

On June 2, 1903, Andersen held a family meeting with his wife and two sons, Fred, seventeen, and Herbert, eighteen. The boys would graduate from high school the next day. Andersen reminded them that he had promised to pay for their college educations. He also pointed out that both boys had expressed an interest in learning business from him. He asked what they wanted to do. Fred and Herbert chose the lumberyard, and two days later they became part of their father's new plans.

Hans Andersen knew from experience that windows caused problems both for builders and homeowners, primarily because no standard window sizes existed in 1903. Carpenters either created window frames while they constructed a building or had them custom built by lumberyards or millwork shops, often with poor results. Andersen recognized the market for high-quality window frames and the benefits of standardization: (1) building owners could enjoy higher-quality windows; (2) carpenters could install them quickly and easily; (3) dealers could carry less inventory; and (4) Andersen could realize the efficiencies of mass production. He ventured into the window industry with three guiding principles for doing business: make a product that is different and better; hire the best people and pay top wages; and provide steady employment insofar as humanly possible.

In 1905 he originated the "two-bundle" method of packaging the pieces of a window frame. One bundle held two horizontal pieces while the other had a pair of vertical pieces. A carpenter could choose the correct sizes for a window opening and install them without cutting or trimming.

Fred Andersen started selling the bundles locally, hauling them around on streetcars in Minneapolis and St. Paul. The company broke even during its first full year of factory operations, but the response was strong. Frame production doubled in 1907, doubled again in 1908, then tripled in 1909. In response to the rapid growth, the family decided to build a new plant, buying land three miles north on the Minnesota side of the St. Croix River in what is now the city of Bayport. One drawback to the new site was the problem of crossing the river, which could be done only by pontoon bridge at Stillwater. Hans Andersen accepted the role of president of the Hudson Bridge Company to actively promote the construction of a new bridge between Hudson and the Minnesota shore.

To further complicate the company's busy schedule, a fire in 1911 destroyed thousands of window-frame parts, hurting sales that year before Andersen Windows rebounded in 1912. The new plant opened in March 1913.

In the spirit of "All together, boys," Hans Andersen called a family meeting to discuss an idea he had heard of called "profit sharing." His plan involved paying the best wages in the industry, setting a reasonable percentage of the profits for investors, then sharing the rest of the profits with employees. The family agreed, and on December 23, 1914, Andersen signed the company's first profit-sharing checks totaling $1,420, an amount equal to 5 percent of his annual payroll. During the train ride to Hudson he felt ill, so he stopped by his doctor's office on the way home. The doctor told him to take it easy for a while and Andersen thanked him for the advice. While walking home he collapsed and died of a heart attack.

The original Andersen plant in Hudson, Wisconsin, 1905. Photograph courtesy of the Andersen Corporation.

Andersen's sons continued to expand the company, building the window busi-
ness while acquiring and running nineteen lumberyards in Minnesota and Wisconsin.
They also continued to share their company's success with its employees, establish-
ing a free life-insurance plan and creating a disability program in 1916. Over time,
Fred Andersen interpreted his father's philosophy of "All together, boys" as the Magic
Circle, which he described in the book of the same name:

> The Magic Circle has eight links. The first is the craftsmanship and skill of Andersen
> workers whose incentive to do fine work is a good wage, a share in profits and other
> tangible benefits. Good management is the second link, providing the capital, preci-
> sion machinery and the finest raw materials to help make quality window products.
> Research engineers constantly developing and improving Andersen products provide
> the third link, and the fourth is the Andersen sales organization, coupling efficient
> promotion and national advertising to move the products from plant to marketplace.
> The fifth link connects millwork distributors and dealers who find the line profitable
> and valuable for repeat business and increasing good will. Builders and architects, pre-
> ferring to use and specify quality window products for enhancement of their reputa-
> tions, are sixth in the chain and the ultimate consumer is the seventh. Since windows
> are one of the four basic essentials of a building, they are willing to pay for quality
> windows. The eighth and deciding link is the premise that in better homes and
> buildings on the one hand—and in a higher standard of living on the other—there is
> a benefit to all members of the Magic Circle, from maker to user.

While the Andersen Corporation embraces the Magic Circle, the connections it
describes capture a prominent Minnesota theme. In addition to the benefits it provides
customers and employees, the company's philanthropy is legendary in the St. Croix
River valley. Theodore Hamm demonstrated a similar concern for his employees, customers, and community. The philanthropy of the Hills, Pillsburys, Daytons, and others continues to serve the common good today. From the cooperative dairy movement
promoted by John Brandt to the medical devices created by Earl Bakken to the college
founded by Sister Antonia McHugh, some of the most enduring enterprises founded
by Minnesota entrepreneurs have succeeded by serving others.

Sister Antonia McHugh

Archbishop John Ireland of St. Paul believed in higher education for women for practical reasons: since they did most of the teaching in public and parochial schools,
one key to increasing the number of Catholic schools was to increase the number of
trained female teachers. In 1890 only two private Minnesota colleges—Hamline University in St. Paul and Carleton College in Northfield—were attracting significant
numbers of women, while only 109 women had earned degrees from the University of
Minnesota between 1869 and 1890. No women's college existed in the state.

Ireland wanted to change that, but his plans to build a women's college in the 1890s were scuttled by the panic of 1893. In 1900 the archbishop tried again, assigning the rights to a special edition of his essays to the Sisters of St. Joseph, who raised $60,000 selling the books. He also persuaded Hugh Derham, a local wheat farmer, to contribute $20,000 to founding the college. The book sales, donation, and a loan enabled the sisters to break ground for their new college's first building, Derham Hall, in 1903.

The College of St. Catherine became one of four Minnesota colleges dedicated solely to the higher education of women. St. Catherine, St. Teresa, St. Scholastica, and St. Benedict all offered classes by 1915, extending a strong entrepreneurial tradition among Catholic sisters in Minnesota that started when the Sisters of St. Francis built St. Marys Hospital in Rochester in 1889.

Classes at the College of St. Catherine began the first week of January 1905. At first, the small preparatory school offered an undefined course of studies to only a handful of women. After nine years of struggling to distinguish itself, the college got a new dean, and a dynamic new direction, in 1914.

Sister Antonia McHugh had been one of twenty-seven sisters who staffed Derham Hall when it had seventy boarders in 1905. McHugh had joined the Sisters of St. Joseph in 1890 at age seventeen, taking permanent vows in 1898. She earned a bachelor's degree from the University of Chicago in 1908 and a master's degree in philosophy in 1909.

Like many of the entrepreneurs featured in this book, McHugh brought vision, dedication, energy, and fearlessness to her work, qualities that began to take shape when she was just four years old. Her father, Patrick McHugh, built the first hotel in the town of Deadwood in the Dakota Territory, only one year after the nearby Battle of the Little Big Horn. Young Anna was the only white girl in town, a distinction that earned her abundant attention from local miners and from Wild West celebrities that included Calamity Jane, Buffalo Bill, and Chief Red Cloud.

Her family moved to Langdon in the Dakota Territory when Anna was nine. Patrick McHugh enjoyed politics, serving in the territorial legislature from 1884 to 1888. He was instrumental in convincing James J. Hill's Great Northern Railway to lay track to Langdon to save area farmers from having to haul their grain seventy-five miles to the nearest railroad. He also helped Langdon become the county seat by persuading nearby settlements to vote for their towns, splitting the vote and leaving Langdon the winner. He became the town's first mayor.

While Anna McHugh learned tenacity and political skills from her father, she acquired her courage, vision, and faith from her mother and from other women she encountered as she grew up. In a radio address in 1933, she said, "The soul of a pioneer woman is a beautiful thing. It is full of wisdom and hope and self-sacrifice. . . . All pioneer women saw visions and dreamed dreams while they were facing the bare realities. They gave courage and endurance to the trailblazers at every step of the way. They had faith in the new land, and faith made them zealous."

Sister Antonia McHugh. Photograph courtesy of the College of St. Catherine Archive.

Her observations reflect the qualities Sister Antonia McHugh brought to her new job as dean of the College of St. Catherine. Faced with problems on several fronts, she followed the advice of a teacher and friend from Chicago to begin by assembling a distinguished faculty, building a substantial library, and expanding and upgrading the curriculum.

Like Minnesota's other Catholic colleges, St. Catherine's could not get accredited because it lacked sufficient endowment funds to financially ensure the school's future. McHugh met with the heads of the other colleges and suggested they convince the North Central Association that the lives of the sisters, who served without pay, represented the equivalent of a cash endowment. The argument worked and the colleges were accredited.

Because the state's Catholic colleges rarely received financial support from the church, McHugh had to seek outside assistance. She became the first women's college leader in Minnesota to ask foundations for support. In 1918 and again in 1921 she secured a $100,000 grant from the Rockefeller Foundation. She continued to solicit grants and gifts to build the college.

McHugh's twenty-five-year plan for the campus featured buildings surrounding a central quadrangle. At one point she displayed her father's political savvy to keep the campus intact. She learned that the city of St. Paul planned to extend Prior Avenue directly through the campus. She immediately traveled to New York to find money for a new building, completed plans for its design, and built and opened Mendel Hall, all in seven months. The building blocked the path of Prior Avenue. To placate the city she built a small side road alongside Mendel Hall, but it was never completed or used.

McHugh cared for the campus as if it were her home, picking up litter, raking leaves, and planting hundreds of trees and thousands of flowers. When the college couldn't afford sod, she filled her habit pockets with grass seed and scattered it while walking and saying her prayers. She had the drive paved with red brick and enclosed the campus with a wrought-iron fence. The college's halls and classrooms displayed paintings, prints, engravings, statues, and antiques she brought back from her trips.

McHugh also cared for the sisters who taught at the college, inspiring them to be learners as well as teachers. She once said, "If you bring a thimble to the fount of knowledge, you'll get a thimbleful; if you bring a pail, you'll get a pail full." She made sure everyone brought a pail, encouraging the sisters to pursue advanced degrees at Catholic University in Washington, D.C., and at secular universities in Illinois, Michigan, and Europe. By 1920 a dozen sisters had received master's degrees. On her trips east she made a point of bringing different sisters with her, giving them the responsibility of paying bills and tips and introducing them to art galleries, concerts, plays, and auctions.

During her twenty-three-year tenure as dean and president of the College of St. Catherine, Sister Antonia McHugh transformed a small preparatory school into a leader in the higher education of women. She resigned the presidency because of

McHugh directed the funding, design, and construction of Mendel Hall (center right), all in seven months. Photograph courtesy of the Minnesota Historical Society.

illness in 1937. Her leadership made St. Catherine's the first Catholic college to be accredited by an official association, the first to educate its sisters in secular universities, the first to have its library school accredited by the American Library Association, and the first to be granted a chapter of Phi Beta Kappa, the collegiate national honor society. More important, she inspired generations of young women to become the kind of leader she was, acting with courage and commitment in the interests of those they served.

William McKnight

Like Antonia McHugh, William McKnight took the reins of a struggling organization and turned it into an enduring enterprise. He too relied upon a keen vision and clear sense of what was right to make Minnesota Mining and Manufacturing a leader in its field. But the similarities end there. While the College of St. Catherine became what it started out to be, 3M was founded to exploit a mineral deposit, became a sandpaper manufacturer to avoid bankruptcy, then relied upon its sensitivity to customer needs to become the world's leading supplier of coated abrasive materials.

William McKnight joined 3M as a young assistant bookkeeper in 1907. Shortly after graduating from high school, he had left his parents' farm in South Dakota to

William McKnight. Photograph courtesy of 3M.

join his sister and her new husband in Duluth. The company had been formed five years earlier near Duluth in Two Harbors, Minnesota, by five businessmen hoping to strike it rich with a mineral they believed was corundum, a valuable abrasive and the hardest metal on earth next to diamonds. A Duluth prospector claimed to have found corundum northeast of Two Harbors near the shores of Lake Superior. Demand in the United States for the two most popular abrasives, corundum and emery, had doubled since 1897 and the only operational corundum mine was in northern Ontario. Sensing a great opportunity, a physician, lawyer, merchant, and two railroad executives formed the Minnesota Mining and Manufacturing Company.

If ignorance is bliss, 3M's first owners had to enjoy those early months. It took nearly a year before they actually tested the mineral's marketability, and when one of the founders reported back that it was "fairly satisfactory," they decided to move forward, unaware that the mineral was not actually corundum, making it unfit for abrasive work. They also did not know that a New York company had developed an artificial abrasive that was rapidly replacing corundum and emery.

Their first sale came nearly two years after they founded the company: one ton of "corundum" for $20. It was to be their only sale in two-and-a-half years. Facing insolvency, lawyer John Dwan, one of the company's founders, wrote to Edgar Ober, a St. Paul railroad officer who owned five thousand shares of 3M stock, describing the critical need for financial help, his doubts that the company could survive selling bulk "corundum," and his idea that the company manufacture its own sandpaper and abrasives instead. The drawback to such a plan, of course, was the cost of setting up an abrasives factory: an estimated $25,000 in addition to the $14,000 3M needed to pay its debts. Dwan offered 60 percent of the company's stock to any investor who would pay the debts and provide working capital until 3M was back on its feet.

Ober took the proposal to a friend, Lucius Pond Ordway, who was vice president of Crane and Ordway, a successful wholesale plumbing-supply firm in St. Paul. Ordway agreed to the offer. By May 1905 Ober and Ordway controlled the company, which they moved to Duluth.

Ordway's initial investment of $25,000 to build the factory grew to $100,000 after a devastating storm destroyed a new dock and warehouse full of "corundum" on Lake Superior. Despite receiving its first orders for sandpaper in 1906, the company continued to lose money. Monthly sales averaging $2,500 fell well short of monthly expenses that averaged $9,000.

The original 3M plant for mining and crushing corundum at Crystal Bay, northeast of Duluth on Lake Superior. Photograph courtesy of 3M.

The company finally made a small profit in 1909, even though the quality of 3M sandpaper was well below that of its competitors' products. Ober and Ordway decided to move the plant to St. Paul in 1910, at which point Ordway's investment in 3M exceeded $250,000. Trouble continued to plague the company at its new site. With the plant completed but the machinery not yet installed, two employees inventoried the raw material available for production, stacking the one-hundred-pound bags eight deep on the first-floor bay. That night the floor gave way, leaving a gaping hole and garnet and flint scattered across the basement.

That same year Ober made William McKnight the sales manager for 3M, despite the young accountant's lack of sales knowledge or experience. McKnight approached the job with a new philosophy: rather than stop at the front office of prospective customers, which was common practice, he met with the end users. Once a month he took the train to Rockford, Illinois, to call on the city's twenty-nine furniture plants. His persistence paid off when managers finally allowed him to meet with the men and women who used sandpaper. McKnight established a system of selling: (1) get into the back shop; (2) talk with the workers to determine the best abrasive for the job; and (3) report complaints to the sales office and provide samples of unsatisfactory sandpaper to the factory.

The third step was a routine part of every sales call because 3M sandpaper rarely achieved the quality of competitive products. Poor quality also cost 3M whenever it actually competed for a sale. Buyers frequently told McKnight that a competitor had offered a discount but that they might buy from 3M if he offered a greater discount. McKnight concluded that the only way 3M would succeed was by making superior products that commanded premium prices, an opinion 3M's directors shared.

Yet quality continued to suffer. On a sales call in Ohio, McKnight demonstrated 3M's garnet-cloth sanding belts to a potential customer. Some belts performed well but others failed, and the lack of uniformity made selling nearly impossible. A frustrated McKnight wrote a letter to Ober recommending the creation of a new position of general manager to oversee both sales and operations. Ober liked the idea and appointed McKnight, who in turn promoted Archibald Bush to the sales manager job. One of their first acts was to stop using the "corundum" mined from the North Shore. It had taken seven years and miles of sandpaper to realize that the mineral they were using, the mineral upon which 3M was founded, was worthless.

Under McKnight's leadership the quality of 3M sandpaper improved, but the company had one more hurdle to overcome. In 1914, the year he became general manager, repeat orders for 3M sandpaper stopped when customers complained that the abrasive fell off the paper after just a few minutes of use. The company studied the problem and scrutinized the production process for weeks but could find no cause. The factory continued to produce sandpaper that failed until a worker noticed an oily film on the water in a scrub pail that held garnet swept from the floor. They knew glue wouldn't stick to an oily surface so they tested samples of the uncrushed garnet and found it was contaminated. Further investigation revealed that the sacks of garnet had crossed the Atlantic on a Spanish tramp steamer that also carried olive oil. When a storm at sea popped the corks on the oil, it seeped into the sacks. No damage was apparent so the incident was never reported. 3M had to thoroughly heat 200 tons of garnet to roast off the oil before they could use the mineral.

At the time, quality testing consisted of the factory superintendent running his thumbnail across the sandpaper before the glue dried to see if the right amount of mineral had been applied. Each 3M sandpaper maker developed his own formulas and designed his own machinery. The lack of a uniform, systematic approach bothered McKnight, who organized 3M's first laboratory for testing raw materials, quality during production, and finished products.

Improvements in quality and customer service helped 3M finally turn the corner in 1914. McKnight struck deals with two distributors to sell 3M abrasives. Archibald Bush believed the distributors would sell more if they understood what they were selling, so he had 3M sales representatives accompany the distributors' people on calls. Not only did the strategy inform the distributors about 3M products, it helped 3M salesmen better understand their customers' needs. Within a year one of the distributors stopped carrying competitors' products. By 1917, fifteen large distributors offered 3M products.

3M's first innovation was the development of an aluminum-oxide cloth for sanding metal parts, primarily for the growing automobile industry. Within three years it became the company's best-selling product line. At the same time, World War I dramatically increased the demand for abrasives. Between the new cloth and the war, 3M's sales volume jumped from $263,000 in 1914 to $1.4 million in 1919.

Two breakthrough products in the early 1920s solidified the success of 3M, both the result of the company culture, initiated and nurtured by William McKnight, of listening to its customers. The first started with a letter McKnight received from a Philadelphia printing-ink manufacturer requesting samples of every mineral grit size 3M used to make sandpaper. The typical response would have been to throw the letter away or pass it along to someone in the factory, but McKnight wondered why a printing-ink manufacturer would want grit. His eastern division sales manager subsequently learned that the letter writer, Francis Okie, was an inventor who had used stationery from his uncle's printing-ink business. A man who beveled glass for a living worked next to the ink business. Watching him, Okie noticed all the glass dust the man was breathing and wondered why someone didn't sell a waterproof abrasive, so he invented one. 3M bought the rights to the sandpaper from Okie in February 1921 and hired Okie to work on new-product design. The waterproof sandpaper, called WETORDRY, was exactly what McKnight had been seeking ever since he realized, as sales manager, that 3M's future depended on making superior products that commanded premium prices.

WETORDRY found a booming market in the auto-painting business. When Dick Drew came to work for 3M after one year of college, he was given the job of taking Okie's WETORDRY samples to St. Paul auto-body refinishing shops for testing. The shops were deluged with people who wanted two-tone paint jobs for their cars. Every time Drew delivered the samples he heard shop workers swearing at the paint as they struggled to get a sharp line between two colors. To protect the parts they didn't want spray painted, workers glued old newspapers to the parts. The glue often stuck too well, ruining the finish when it was removed, or it didn't stick well enough and allowed paint to seep through.

In his youthful exuberance Drew promised a solution with no idea what it would be. 3M gave him permission to find one. After three years of experimentation he could offer only a poor-quality tape that McKnight refused to sell. Drew returned to his job helping Okie but his mind remained on the tape. As he was fetching a roll of crimped towel-type paper for Okie, Drew wondered if the paper might solve his tape problem. He tested it and it worked. After further experimentation and refinement, Drew created 3M's signature product, Scotch-brand cellophane tape, in 1930.

Through the leadership of William McKnight, who was the company's general manager, president, and board chair until he retired in 1966, 3M emerged from more than a dozen years of adversity to become an enduring enterprise. McKnight turned the company around by tirelessly advocating three values that continue to define 3M today: promote innovation, produce superior products, and respond to customer needs.

Charles Beckman

For twenty-two years Charles Beckman sold shoes at his retail store in Red Wing, Minnesota. After selling more than a half-million shoes and boots, he had extensive firsthand knowledge of what his customers needed. Too often, to his frustration, Beckman did not have the right size or type shoe for his customers. That frustration and a restless spirit led to the founding of the Red Wing Shoe Company.

Beckman's teenage journey from his native Germany to the United States got off to a rocky start when his boat was shipwrecked off the coast of Halifax, England. Undeterred, Beckman headed west and ended up in Red Wing, where, in 1873, he got a job at Trout Brook Tannages. The owner of the tannery, S. B. Foot, had opened the town's first shoe company in 1861. Shoemaking demanded leather so Foot opened a tannery. Beckman worked at the tannery for ten years before deciding to open a shoe store with Foot's financial support.

By 1900 Red Wing had become a manufacturing center that included the tannery, several sawmills, two pottery makers, and factories that produced hats, gloves, and sewer pipes. Most were started with local money and thrived on local support. Beckman tapped into that support with an advertisement in the local newspaper announcing his new venture: "I am Beckman the Shoe Man. I have been spending the greater part of my life supplying the people of this community with shoes and boots. I am now about to quit selling shoes because I have commenced making them."

Beckman incorporated the Red Wing Shoe Company in February 1905 with six local businessmen, including S. B. Foot. Twenty community members quickly snapped up a capital stock offering of $100,000. Beckman focused on making high-quality work shoes for men and boys, producing 110 pairs of shoes in a ten-hour day. An apprentice system trained workers in their new trade, paying them $2 for a fifty-nine-hour week their first year, $3 a week their second year, and $6 a week their third year, after which they became shoe cutters paid $16.50 a week in gold. Demand proved strong from the start because of the need for well-made work shoes, a need Beckman had recognized as a shoe salesman. He promoted his shoes to the local community, advertising, "We want every man and boy to wear Red Wing made shoes." Costs ranged from $1.75 to $3 a pair for men's shoes and $1.50 to $2 for boys' shoes.

Beckman's initial sales territory included all of Minnesota and parts of Iowa and Nebraska. He and two other traveling salesmen worked the territory. In 1907 Beckman was aboard a Great Western train headed for Kansas City when it collided with another train near Marshalltown, Iowa. As with the shipwreck thirty-five years earlier, Beckman survived, but he lost his shoe samples. Instead of returning home he went to Des Moines, where he knew he could sell shoes without the samples.

By 1909 the Red Wing Shoe Company employed one hundred people. Beckman made several trips to Chicago to persuade the big mail-order houses to carry his shoes but they turned him down, a disappointment that proved to be beneficial to the company because it could continue to focus on quality without the compromises that higher volumes from the mail-order houses almost certainly would have created.

Charles Beckman retired because of poor health in 1911, but his commitment to quality and customer service, like that of 3M's William McKnight, had shaped an enduring enterprise that continues to excel today.

The cutting-room floor at the Red Wing Shoe Company. Photograph courtesy of the Red Wing Shoe Company.

H. M. Byllesby

Like Charles Beckman, Henry Marison Byllesby learned his industry for more than twenty years before founding a company that would become a Minnesota icon. When he changed the name of his growing business to Northern States Power in 1916, Byllesby recognized that the acquisitions he continued to make would produce a dominant regional utility.

He had formed the Washington County Light and Power Company in 1909, buying Stillwater Gas and Electric less than two months later. Byllesby understood that connecting more communities with electrical service meant benefits for the utility through the mass production of power and for the consumer through lower rates and more dependable service. Within five years he had a network comprised of Faribault, Mankato, Northfield, Coon Rapids, Rockford, Delano, Watertown, Waconia, Chaska, Shakopee, and Crookston, as well as Grand Forks, North Dakota. The number of customers grew from a few thousand to forty-eight thousand in 1912 and eighty-one thousand in 1915, at which point Byllesby added lines around the Twin Cities linking Minneapolis, St. Paul, Chaska, and Shakopee.

After World War I, the utility industry underwent dramatic consolidation. Within eight years 3,744 public utilities ceased to exist because of merger or acquisition. One percent of the country's utility corporations ended up owning 84 percent of all utility assets. Byllesby made sure Northern States Power thrived by spearheading the acquisition of forty-two companies in just seven years.

Contrary to popular wisdom, which held that power should be made near where it was used, Byllesby believed utilities should generate power at a favorable location, then transmit it to customers over many miles. His concept quickly became the dominant approach in the industry. He also believed that everyone had the right to electricity, an unpopular notion among competitors who thought it was too expensive to connect farmers to the system. At first, the farmers Byllesby hooked up used too little electricity to justify the expense. Rather than stopping their service, Northern States Power decided to convince farmers of electricity's value to their chores. Midwest universities and colleges and electrical-equipment manufacturers joined NSP to devise ideas and prototypes for electric milking machines, cream separators, water pumps, corn huskers, and other machines. Farmers who tried the machines discovered they made more money and had more free time as a result, benefits that ensured the electrification of rural Minnesota.

H. M. Byllesby learned to think creatively from a master. Thomas Edison hired Byllesby, who had just earned his engineering degree, to help build Manhattan's Pearl Street electrical station in 1881. Byllesby ended up drawing every structure, crane, boiler location, engine, and electric switchboard for the station. In 1885 George Westinghouse hired him to manage the Westinghouse Electric Company. Not only did he organize and manage the business, over a four-year period Byllesby invented at least forty electric lighting devices for his new plant to manufacture.

Henry Marison Byllesby. Photograph courtesy of the Xcel Energy Corporation.

He came to St. Paul in 1891 to run a subsidiary of Thomson-Houston Electric Company. He paid close attention to the local power industry, admiring how Governor Alexander Ramsey's St. Paul Gas Light Company took on all competitors in a rapidly expanding market while recognizing that those who struggled and failed typically lacked money, engineering ability, and courage.

Byllesby used what he learned to establish an engineering and operating firm in Chicago, buying, rehabilitating, and building public utility properties in Minnesota, the Dakotas, Wisconsin, Oklahoma, California, and Alabama. He returned to Minnesota in 1909 to organize the Washington County Light and Power Company, which evolved into NSP.

To make sure his company avoided the unscrupulous tactics that plagued his industry, Byllesby wrote and distributed a code of business ethics. In part, it advised all employees to "deal honestly . . . lawfully. Charge the lowest possible rates. Keep the cards on the table. We want no secret deals . . . take the people into your confidence.

An early Northern States Power generating plant. Photograph courtesy of the Xcel Energy Corporation.

Give them the facts. Maintain the old-fashioned virtues. They will always win in the long run."

"Old-fashioned virtues" guided the attitudes and actions of Minnesota's leading entrepreneurs at the turn of the century. Theodore Hamm, for instance, helped establish German communities in St. Paul by treating the farmers he bought grain from, the employees he worked alongside, and the customers he sold beer and meat to with honesty and respect. It is hard to imagine a leader today encouraging his employees to form a union, and it's even less likely that the employees would want to make that leader their union president.

As they did for Hamm, the virtues of cooperation and mutual support helped Hans Andersen create his enduring enterprise. As a young man he learned that the most difficult tasks, such as prying up deep-rooted tree stumps, could be accomplished when everyone pulled together. As an entrepreneur, his "All together, boys" philosophy meant unusual loyalty to his employees, first as a mill operator in St. Cloud and Hudson and then as the founder of Andersen Corporation. The generous profit-sharing checks Andersen's employees continue to receive today reinforce the value all workers have in "the Magic Circle."

Sister Antonia McHugh valued beauty, courage, and persistence, virtues that allowed a fledgling college to flourish. In her pursuit of knowledge—for herself, her Sisters, and her students—she strove for excellence, constantly moving toward her vision of what the College of St. Catherine could become.

For those who doubt the value of "old-fashioned virtues," the experience of 3M offers compelling evidence. Before William McKnight took charge of the company, it was notorious for the poor quality of its products. McKnight made quality and service the foundation of the company and its fortunes turned. The innovative spirit that still defines 3M today began with creative approaches to solving customer problems with high-quality products. For 3M, service and quality made good business sense.

The same can be said for George Draper Dayton, the man who turned a struggling dry-goods store into a business that became synonymous with shopping in Minnesota.

George Draper Dayton

George Dayton never dreamed of running a department store, nor could he have imagined he would make his mark in Minnesota. In the summer of 1873, he passed the entrance exams for Hobart College, where he intended to enroll in the fall to become a minister. First, however, amid the panic of 1873, Dayton and his brother took jobs as "budders" at George McMillan's nursery, about thirty miles south of their home in Geneva, New York. Returning home in September to begin college, he learned that his father had arranged a full-time job for him with McMillan at a salary of $800 a year plus room and board, plus a commission on all sales beyond a certain amount. True to his adaptable nature, Dayton figured he would work before going to college. (The fact that he was rooming across the street from Emma Chadwick, a young woman he would later marry, surely made the change in plans more palatable.)

Young Dayton worked hard. "Mr. McMillan had no idea I would get any commission," Dayton wrote in his autobiography, "but I was ambitious and I used the evenings to solicit sales. At the end of the year $800 in commissions were due me. I had drawn very little of the salary, so around $1500 were due and Mr. McMillan could not pay. He suggested I buy the coal and lumberyard." His parents advised against it, but Dayton wanted the money he had earned. He convinced his father to give him

George Draper Dayton. Used by permission of the Target Corporation.

$2,000 that had been set aside for college and became the owner of the business. He was seventeen years old and $7,000 in debt—an amount roughly equal to $110,000 in 2001.

Dayton wanted to marry, but felt he could not until he was twenty-one and had saved $5,000. His strategy for acquiring the money reflected a youthful ambition unfettered by common sense: In the winter of 1876–1877, he worked every other night, all night long. By spring he was exhausted. His father sold the business and Dayton rested until summer, when he had fully recovered. He took a job helping John Mackay with his lumberyard, sawmill, and other ventures. Within four years Dayton was in charge of Mackay's office and banking business. Wise investment of the proceeds from the sale of his own business allowed Dayton to save $5,000 by his twenty-first birthday, and he married Emma Chadwick on December 17, 1878. The couple made a habit of setting aside $5 every Saturday night. "We bought nothing on the installment plan, we had no charge accounts, we paid cash for all we bought," Dayton later wrote. Their savings and Dayton's financial responsibilities for Mackay played key roles in George and Emma Dayton ending up in Minnesota.

By 1881 several prominent citizens of Geneva had invested in the promise of the Midwest, holding mortgages on land in and around Worthington, Minnesota. They had been persuaded to invest in Worthington by Thomas Parsons, owner of the Bank of Worthington, who had connections with investors in the Geneva area. When these investors, who included George and Emma Dayton, could not get satisfactory answers from Parsons about their investments, they sent Dayton to Minnesota to investigate in November 1881.

Although the grasshopper plague of the mid-1870s and the effects of the panic of 1873 had ended, life in southwestern Minnesota remained difficult. The bitter winter of 1880–81 delayed trains to the area, creating a fuel shortage that forced farmers to burn hay to stay warm. Unable to pay their mortgages, many farmers fled. Looters took doors, windows, floors, and whatever else they could carry from the abandoned farms. Dayton observed the situation and, upon returning to Geneva, recommended that investors put someone who represented their interests in Worthington. A return trip the following year only confirmed his advice. The investors proposed that Dayton buy the Bank of Worthington and take possession in April 1883. Despite the problems, he saw the area's potential and decided to make his home in Worthington. The experience and confidence he had gained while running his own business as a youth surely influenced his decision, since he knew nothing about banking. While learning the business from associates in Geneva, he appealed to potential investors to put more money into southwestern Minnesota. Many responded, often only because they trusted Dayton.

For the next nineteen years George Dayton helped settle Worthington and the area around it, understanding that a community needed people to flourish and doing his best to attract and keep them. In his autobiography he told the story of a man with five children who had moved to town to run a dray. Dayton advised him that he had a better future farming his own land, which he could start by purchasing a quarter-section of land for $50 down and $50 a year. The man said he didn't have $50 so Dayton waived that requirement. The man said he would need $200 to repair the existing farm buildings and Dayton gave it to him, adding the amount to the loan. The man then said he would need ten cows to make a decent start and Dayton said he would pay for them, again adding the price to the loan. "He went, and made good," Dayton wrote.

He ended up in Minneapolis when the investment company he started decided to divide its risks between the country and the city. Dayton looked into Chicago, Kansas City, Denver, and St. Paul before choosing Minneapolis by standing on street corners and counting people. Although most commerce at that time was conducted "downtown," nearer the flour mills and river, his research convinced him to confine his buying to Nicollet Avenue between Fourth and Tenth Streets, the "uptown" area many merchants considered too far from the action.

Dayton bought, sold, and traded land easily. In addition to lots in residential areas of Minneapolis, he worked tirelessly to acquire the land at Seventh and Nicollet. By 1901 he owned enough of the property to construct a six-story building on the site. His search for a lead tenant for the new building led him to the R. S. Goodfellow Company, the fourth-largest department store in the city. Dayton believed that locating Goodfellow in his building would attract shoppers uptown, an early vision of the anchor concept Dayton's department store would later deploy at its suburban shopping malls known as the Dales. He became a silent partner with the store's two owners, renting the space and providing $50,000 of the necessary capital in exchange for rent and dividends as a stockowner. Goodfellow opened its Daylight Store in Dayton's new building in June 1902, the same month that his oldest son, Draper, graduated from Princeton. Within a year father and son would be running the department store.

The Goodfellow Company more than doubled its business that first year. George Dayton bought out one of the company's partners after discovering unscrupulous financial dealings, then the other shortly thereafter. "It was very risky," he wrote, "but really there was nothing for us to do but go ahead with the store. We lost money, but we gained experience. I kept track of losses until they passed $100,000. Then I said, 'I don't want to know the loss. We are going to make this win,' and the result speaks for itself." Although sales continued to grow, the store did not realize a profit until 1906. Dayton aggressively pursued profitability, offering company stock to employees, changing the store's name to Dayton's, and expanding the store's size and services in 1903. For his part, Draper Dayton rejected the popular notion that a store must cater to one class of customers, leading eventually to a basement store in 1909 that offered lower prices. George Dayton made his son the store's general manager in 1906, maintaining a regular presence in the store without interfering in how his son managed it.

Along with the virtues of honesty, quality, and service, George Dayton believed in discipline. Discipline served him well when he and his wife diligently set aside $5 every week even though they had not completely furnished their home, and it served

The original Dayton's building in downtown Minneapolis in 1902. Used by permission of the Target Corporation.

him well as the leader of a growing enterprise. When a meeting was scheduled to begin, he would close the door to the room, allowing no latecomers to enter.

Dayton continued to expand his real-estate holdings until, in 1910, his company owned the entire frontage to Nicollet Avenue between Seventh and Eighth streets. The following year, in an effort to expand leadership, he persuaded Draper's brother, Nelson, to become a partner in the business. Under their leadership the store flourished, surviving World War I and a spirited competition with rival department store Donaldsons. Dayton's also overcame a fire in 1917 that destroyed up to a half-million dollars' worth of shoes and damaged much of the store's remaining stock. In 1922 it held its first Jubilee sale, increasing merchandise and slashing prices. The sale exceeded all expectations and made Dayton's the leading department store in the city.

In July 1923, Draper Dayton died suddenly of heart failure at the age of forty-three. Heartbroken, George Dayton wanted to sell the store but agreed to support Nelson Dayton's decision to keep it. While his son resolved to build a strong executive team, George Dayton became more involved with the store. He made it a habit to speak to employees in what he called "store talks," explaining policies, providing background for new employees, giving advice, and discussing economic trends. During his travels he often took the time to benchmark other department stores, reporting his findings to his son by letter.

In the summer of 1929 the Dayton Company bought the J. B. Hudson Company, and George Dayton, at age seventy-two, became president of the jewelry retailer. Despite the stock market crash later that year, the Dayton Hudson Department Store Company continued to show a profit, although the aftermath of the crash strained Dayton financially, largely because he and his wife had given so much of their money to the Dayton Foundation.

In 1909 George and Emma Dayton had established an endowment fund for the future Dayton Foundation with a pledge of $500,000. The foundation was incorporated in 1918 with $900,000 contributed by the Daytons plus title to the land upon which the Dayton's store sat, leased to the Dayton Company for $50,000 a year.

The Daytons took great pleasure in giving money to support others. By 1926 George Dayton estimated that he and his wife had already given away $5 million. He continued to actively participate in the foundation's efforts until his death in 1938. In his autobiography he wrote, "I have been favored with the kind assistance of many— and I have endeavored to pass on to others, recognizing that 'From them to whom much is given much shall (properly) be required.'"

One of the causes championed by George Dayton and the Dayton Foundation was the YMCA. In December 1927 he spoke at the YMCA, capturing the essence of his entrepreneurial spirit—and that of Hans Andersen, Sister Antonia McHugh, William McKnight, and others—in his closing remarks:

> That is the great thought that I desire you to get tonight. (1) That life is full of little opportunities; (2) That doing well, doing splendidly all these little things will make our lives a success. And, when we go, people will miss us not because we built up a fortune, but because we made those about us happier, more comfortable and enriched the world with our spirit of cheer, optimism, good will and good deeds.

Surviving and Thriving (1915–1940)

Merritt Osborn

One could argue that anyone able to sell a product called Digesto would excel at any business he or she chose. Shortly after opening its new St. Paul brewery in 1894, the Theodore Hamm Brewing Company hired Merritt Osborn to promote Digesto, its medicinal malt extract. Osborn not only sold it, he developed national distribution for the product. His achievement earned him the position of advertising manager for Hamm's, and he became the president of the St. Paul Advertising Club.

But he was restless. In 1910, at the age of thirty-one, Osborn left Hamm's to run his own business. After the end of World War I and the failure of three ventures, Osborn became the Northwest distributor for the Ford Motor Company. Henry Ford had been mass-producing cars for more than a decade, and since the only way to benefit from the efficiencies of an assembly line was to keep it running, he turned out a steady stream of new cars regardless of demand. Dealers and distributors absorbed the cost of mass production by maintaining a bloated inventory, a financial burden that eventually forced Osborn out of business.

Down to his last $5,000, Osborn did not give up on his dream of starting a successful business. He reviewed his life experiences back to his years as a traveling salesman and remembered how the hotels in which he stayed had to keep rooms out of service while the carpets were removed and cleaned, a process that could take up to two weeks. Sensing an opportunity, he talked with several hotel managers to better understand their professional needs, then hired a chemist to formulate a product that cleaned carpets right on the floor. The year was 1923, and with no experience in the business and little working capital, the forty-four-year-old Osborn opened his new

The home-office staff of Economics Laboratory in 1935, with Merritt Osborn seated in the center, flanked by sons E. B. on his right and Steve on his left. Photograph courtesy of Ecolab, Inc.

company, Economics Laboratory, in St. Paul. The chemist came up with Absorbit, a cleaner that did exactly what Osborn hoped and hotel managers desired. Yet demand for the new product never materialized and profits were slight.

Undeterred, Osborn turned his attention to commercial kitchens, where he identified the need for an effective cleaner for mechanized dishwashers. His second product, Soilax, proved more successful than Absorbit, but the cost of research and development and the time required to create the new product strained his financial resources. He also would not allow the product to be introduced unless it could fulfill its sales promise of getting the job done. His high standards combined with his struggle to establish markets for unproven products depleted the company's bank account to the point where Osborn had a stack of bills and no money to pay them.

He decided to sell stock in his company at $50 a share. For weeks he called on everyone he knew and many he didn't, but no one was interested. He finally found a St. Paul investor willing to buy $5,000 in stock and to refer Osborn to a friend, who

A delivery truck advertised Soilax in Chicago in the 1930s. Photograph courtesy of Ecolab, Inc.

also invested $5,000, which convinced others to back Economics Laboratory. The influx of capital turned the company around. In 1928 it introduced its first product dispenser, a milestone in the "total systems" approach to cleaning and sanitation: products and the equipment to dispense them. That same year Osborn's son graduated from college and joined the company. E. B. Osborn's efforts as sales manager for the growing firm helped Economics Laboratory survive the Great Depression. Father and son expanded markets, advertising, and product lines during the 1930s. By 1939 sales reached the half-million-dollar mark, the company paid its third annual cash dividend, and the enduring enterprise later renamed Ecolab was firmly entrenched. Merritt Osborn turned the presidency over to E. B. in 1950.

As Minnesota's early entrepreneurs demonstrated, any point in history holds the capacity for triumph or tragedy. Financial panics dashed plans and stalled recoveries. Natural disasters destroyed years of hard work. New technologies delivered a competitive advantage or took that advantage away. Rich global markets brought with them new levels of uncertainty and anxiety.

No generation of entrepreneurs experienced the roller-coaster ride of dramatic historical events more than those who started their companies in Osborn's era, a period bracketed by two world wars and defined by a decade of unparalleled growth followed by a decade of debilitating financial depression.

Although World War I ended in 1919 and a short recession followed, the energizing influence of the war economy jump-started the Roaring Twenties. Between 1920 and 1929, Minnesotans, like most Americans, used credit to quintuple their purchasing power. And purchase they did. Sophisticated advertising persuaded people to buy

Research and development at Economics Laboratory in 1938. Photograph courtesy of the Minnesota Historical Society.

cars and radios, acquire the latest kitchen gadgets, put pesticides on their lawns and fields, and spend whatever it took to get what they wanted. Leisure time expanded as the workweek shrunk from sixty hours to forty-eight.

For the first time, people considered play as important as work, and they played hard. The adventures of North Pole explorer Richard Byrd, desert traveler T. E. Lawrence, and aviator Charles Lindbergh captivated people. In every field, legendary leaders emerged: writers such as William Faulkner, Ernest Hemingway, and Minnesota's Sinclair Lewis and F. Scott Fitzgerald; entertainers such as Irving Berlin and Will Rogers; artists such as Ansel Adams, Georgia O'Keeffe, and Pablo Picasso; musicians such as Louis Armstrong, Duke Ellington, and George Gershwin; and athletes such as Babe Ruth, Jack Dempsey, Red Grange, and Bobby Jones.

Minnesota's economy underwent an equally dramatic change during the 1920s. Two of its three major industries, lumbering and flour milling, ceased to dominate the commercial landscape. Other industries emerged in their place. Radio broadcast-ing got a big boost in Minnesota in 1920 when Warren G. Harding became the first president ever to speak over the radio, which he did at the Minnesota State Fair. Stan-ley Hubbard launched Hubbard Broadcasting in 1923 when he bought radio station WAMD, which he later renamed KSTP. WCCO Radio began in 1924.

During the 1920s several food-processing plants were built in Minnesota and the meatpacking industry flourished. Washburn-Crosby first marketed Wheaties in 1924; the brand became a household word largely through radio advertising.

Farmers finally realized the full power of the cooperative model in the 1920s. Cooperatives—farmers uniting to market their products through a formal business group—were deeply rooted in Minnesota's agricultural tradition, especially in the dairy business. In 1915 half of the cooperative creameries in the United States existed in Minnesota. Many of these cooperatives had joined forces in 1911 to share informa-tion and coordinate marketing, but much of the profit for their products still went to middlemen. The cooperative creameries sold high-quality butter to dealers in New York and Philadelphia, who then packaged and sold it under various brand names. Consumers who never knew if their butter came from Minnesota had no loyalty to the state's dairy products. At the same time, those who bought butter from several sources had to evaluate every tub of butter because of variations in quality and uni-formity from the dealers. The opportunity begged for an entrepreneur when John Brandt decided to act.

John Brandt

In 1921 John Brandt helped organize a meeting in St. Paul of more than half of Minne-sota's 622 dairy cooperatives. The group decided to form the Minnesota Cooperative Creameries Association with the goal of helping creameries sell their butter. The local cooperatives and individual producers became owners and members of the larger association with a say in its policy decisions and direction and a share of its profits. This cooperative structure continues today.

John Brandt became the association's first president. One of his first acts was to convince the board and member creameries of the profitability in directly selling butter

4-H members recognize Land O'Lakes president John Brandt for his support of 4-H, 1936. Photograph courtesy of the Minnesota Historical Society.

Farmers' cooperatives such as this one in Milaca, Minnesota, circa 1910, helped farmers market their products more effectively. Photograph by Palmquist. Courtesy of the Minnesota Historical Society.

Butter packing at the Minnesota Cooperative Creamery in 1925. Photograph courtesy of the Minnesota Historical Society.

as a group rather than as individual creameries. While the creameries considered the proposal, private dealers threatened not to handle the creameries' butter if they signed the association's marketing agreement. Brandt countered with a series of meetings in 1923 that persuaded nearly 300 creameries to agree to the plan.

Brandt traveled throughout the country to directly contact the association's customers—grocers and distributors—and enlighten them about the quality of Minnesota butter. He soon realized that marketing would be easier if the association's sweet-cream butter had a memorable name. In February 1924 the association announced a contest to name the butter, with a prize of $500 in gold for the winning entry. A panel of judges that included Governor J. A. O. Preus chose Land O'Lakes, which became the association's name in 1926.

The new name and a national marketing campaign led to annual sales of $52 million by the end of the decade. Land O'Lakes opened packaging plants in Duluth and Chicago, handling over ninety-one million pounds of butter a year, and expanded into the egg and turkey businesses. Although sales volume declined after the depression, Land O'Lakes survived through high-quality products, innovative marketing, and diversification. Like the other enduring enterprises that outlasted the depression, Land O'Lakes acquired a resilience that helped it persevere during a world war and thrive in the prosperous times that followed.

J. A. O. Preus and Herman Ekern

As the newly elected governor of Minnesota, J. A. O. Preus had been influential in the 1921 formation of the Minnesota Cooperative Creameries Association. A conservative Republican, he had campaigned in support of cooperation and against "state socialism." The association's goals aligned with his political position, encouraging him to pledge the state's support of the new organization. Preus's own cooperative and entrepreneurial experiences shaped his opinions: in 1918 he and Herman Ekern led the creation of a mutual insurance company that would become Lutheran Brotherhood. It was a feat that required all the political skills both men could muster.

Jacob Aall Otteson Preus and Herman Ekern were prominent Norwegians in a part of the country where Norwegians flourished. By 1930 approximately eight hundred thousand people had immigrated to the United States from Norway, a higher percentage of its homeland population than any other country but Ireland. The majority settled in the Upper Midwest.

Preus grew up in a Lutheran family in which serving the church was the highest honor. Much to his family's dismay, he chose to become a lawyer rather than a man of the cloth, graduating from the University of Minnesota law school in 1906. (Even after Preus became governor of Minnesota, his father commented that he couldn't be prouder of his son—unless, of course, he had been a minister.) Before Preus could open a law practice, however, he got a phone call from Minnesota senator Knute Nelson offering him a job. Nelson was having trouble corresponding with his Norwegian

Herman Ekern (seated, center) and J. A. O. Preus (seated, second from right). Photograph from
A Common Bond: the Story of the Lutheran Brotherhood. Courtesy of the Minnesota Historical
Society.

constituents and wondered if Preus knew shorthand. Preus said he did and took the job,
which he promised to start when he returned from his honeymoon. He then bought
a book on shorthand, which he knew nothing about, read it cover to cover, and spent
much of his honeymoon having his wife help him hone his new shorthand skills.

Senator Nelson became Governor Nelson and, impressed with Preus's abilities,
named Preus Minnesota's commissioner of insurance in 1910. Preus knew little more
about insurance than he had about shorthand, but he studied the subject diligently.
In fact, neither he nor anyone in his family had ever owned life insurance until Preus
bought a policy after becoming commissioner. When his term expired in 1912, he became state auditor.

Like Preus, Herman Ekern was a law-school graduate and insurance commissioner, having graduated from the University of Wisconsin law college and been elected
Wisconsin's insurance commissioner in 1911. Unlike Preus, Ekern practiced law as a
district attorney, sold insurance, and lent money for farm mortgages. In 1902 he was
elected to the state assembly, becoming speaker in 1907. As a state representative,
Ekern made insurance reform a priority, leading the effort to enact better insurance
laws. He became deputy insurance commissioner in 1909 before being elected commissioner and initiated the first system of state life insurance in the nation.

In June 1917 three thousand delegates came to St. Paul to unite three Norwegian-

Lutheran church bodies. Preus and Ekern, who had met when they were insurance commissioners, attended the convention. The leaders of the new Norwegian Lutheran Church of America asked the two men to explore the formation of a committee to study the advisability of a mutual-aid society. They were to report their findings at the convention. The subject triggered intense opinions among the delegates. On the one hand, Progressive reforms had convinced many of the value of and need for insurance. On the other hand, theologically conservative delegates believed that insurance was incompatible with faith in God. Preus had witnessed the fervor of this belief when Norwegian Lutherans questioned his Christianity after he became insurance commissioner.

Despite the opposition, both Preus and Ekern knew that a mutual-aid society for Norwegian Lutherans was important, and their committee drafted a proposal that Preus read to the delegates. The proposal did not use the word "insurance" once. Nevertheless, as soon as the floor opened for questions, an elderly man quoted from the Bible before concluding, "The word of God is my only insurance." Preus countered with the benefits of such a society, quoting from the Bible himself to bolster his position. The delegates unanimously approved the creation of a mutual-aid society. Ekern immediately wrote a preamble and nine articles of incorporation. The committee decided to base the new society in Minneapolis and call it Luther Union.

To be licensed by the state, the society had until October 1918 to secure at least five hundred paid life-insurance applications, each providing coverage of at least $1,000. They met the goal by summer but lacked the capital required to back the policies. Their application for a $6,000 loan was declined by one bank before another granted it, and Luther Union received its Minnesota life-insurance license in September 1918. It had $676,000 of insurance in force and assets of $6,735 when, in the fall of 1918, a flu epidemic swept the country, threatening insurance companies like Luther Union that lacked deep reserves. Fortunately for the new society, it had only one death claim that autumn.

In 1920 Luther Union became the insurance auxiliary of the Lutheran Brotherhood of America, changing its name to Lutheran Brotherhood and opening the sale of insurance to all Lutherans. Preus and Ekern remained involved in the company, with Preus named chair of the board in 1917, a position he held till his death in 1961, and Ekern becoming Lutheran Brotherhood's president in 1929. Despite the depression, Ekern continued a practice he had started early in his career, making sure the company helped farmers by lending them money for their mortgages. Lutheran Brotherhood also established a policy of lending money to churches at a time when Lutheran congregations found it difficult to borrow. In 2001 Lutheran Brotherhood merged with Aid Association for Lutherans to form Thrivent Financial for Lutherans.

Lutheran Brotherhood, Land O'Lakes, and Economics Laboratory became enduring enterprises as they expanded into regional and national markets. These markets became available through magazine and radio advertising and through a growing transportation network. Transcontinental railroads carried freight to every part of a growing nation. Ford trucks sold by Merritt Osborn and other distributors helped manufacturers get their products to ever-broadening markets. As car ownership grew and the number of people on the roads increased, billboard advertising put products and services in front of a mobile society.

The allure of travel and mobility spawned more than one Minnesota enterprise, including Carl Wickman's Greyhound Bus Company.

Carl Wickman

At the urging of a friend, Carl Wickman left Sweden at age seventeen to travel to Arizona. He used all his money for a train ticket from New York to Tucson, Arizona, only to find that his friend had left town. Wickman knew no one, had no money, and spoke no English, but he managed to find a job at a sawmill. He heard stories about all the Swedes in Hibbing, Minnesota, and saved his money for a train ticket north.

Wickman worked as a diamond-drill operator in Iron Range mines, but the frequent layoffs disrupted his income and kept him from marrying and raising a family. In 1913, at the age of twenty-six, he left the mines and bought the local Goodyear tire and Hupmobile dealership, showing the seven-passenger car to everyone he could but making no sales. After a few frustrating months he devised a new plan, buy-

Greyhound officers in 1937, including Carl Wickman (second from left) and Orville Caeser (third from left). Photograph courtesy of the Minnesota Historical Society.

ing the Hupmobile with the $600 he had saved and using it to transport miners to nearby towns. He charged fifteen cents for a one-way trip and a quarter for the round-trip. With gasoline selling for four cents a gallon he made money on every trip, especially when eager miners unable to get a seat rode on the running boards. Wickman established a regular schedule, launching one of the first "bus" routes in the Upper Midwest.

Despite the demand for his service, Wickman was soured by the downside of the business and he sold it for $1,200 to two local fellows the following summer. The car's flapping curtains did little to keep out the cold of winter. Blizzards made driving perilous, while frequent flat tires meant operating a hand pump in the cold and snow while his passengers swore at the delay. When miners refused to pay, which happened often, Wickman fought them for what was due. Although he won far more fights than he lost, he did not plan to endure another winter on the road.

His plans changed. Only one of the two men who bought the business could drive and quickly tired of the work. They asked Wickman to consider rejoining the business with the understanding that he could now split duties with the driving partner. Feeling responsible for the business he had started, Wickman bought out the non-driving partner for $600.

In 1915, their first full year, the two partners earned $8,000, an amount they

Wickman's Hupmobile, used to transport passengers between Alice and Hibbing, Minnesota. Photograph courtesy of the Minnesota Historical Society.

doubled the following year. Success bred competition: a local cab driver named Ralph Bogan decided to drive people back and forth to Duluth, a ninety-mile trip one way on a narrow, rutted road. In the winter Bogan gave his passengers blankets and hot-brick foot warmers, and the hardy miners braved the cold for the attractions of Duluth. As Wickman's business grew, he and his partner decided to buy a second car and modify it with a larger body to hold more passengers. They needed financing and approached Bogan about consolidating their businesses. He agreed with the plan, and two other friends with cars also joined the company. By 1918 they had eighteen cars and an annual income of $40,000.

Wickman entertained bigger plans. At the end of World War I he sold his share of the business for $60,000 and moved to Duluth. He envisioned a network of buses connecting nearby towns and visited with the owners of local bus lines about the possibility, buying shares in those he thought had the most promise. One of his first investments involved a Superior, Wisconsin, company owned by Orville Caeser, with whom Wickman then bought several local lines under the name Motor Transit Corporation. They learned that people traveling from town to town suffered the aggravation of having to remove their luggage, switch vehicles, pay additional fares, and wait for the next bus. The concept of a single network of lines offering one through-ticket became their goal.

Once again expansion required capital, and once again Wickman teamed with Bogan. They expanded aggressively. Small operators joined the growing network because of the economies of scale Wickman offered. Motor Transit paid the cost of bus maintenance, garages, advertising, wages, insurance, and taxes, not to mention the cost of new buses, which General Motors was selling for $13,500. Bogan went to Detroit and negotiated a long-term contract to buy GM buses for $10,000 apiece. Wickman saved money on tires—and on the cost of storing them—by renting them, then exchanging them for new tires after twenty-five thousand miles. He also arranged a discount on gasoline with Texaco and Standard Oil. Finding drivers proved a difficult task, especially when these early drivers had to endure frequent bus breakdowns and weather-related hazards. Those able to endure found themselves in leadership positions as the company grew.

And grow it did. At one point in the Roaring Twenties, Wickman and his partners bought sixty bus lines in six weeks. The rapid growth of bus service caught the railroads' attention and they started buying bus lines to eliminate the competition. In 1928, Louis Hill's last year at the helm of the Great Northern Railway, Wickman and his partners sold 80 percent of Motor Transit's stock to Hill's railroad for $240,000. Their arrangement did not prohibit the bus company from expanding into other parts of the country, which it did vigorously, including the purchase of its chief competitor, Yelloway, for $6.4 million. Since many of the companies Motor Transit bought used the word "greyhound" in their names, in 1930 the company changed its name to the Greyhound Corporation and moved its headquarters from Duluth to Chicago.

In their haste to develop a network Wickman and his partners had overextended

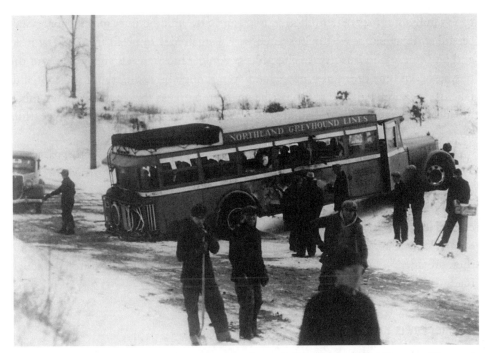

Digging out a Greyhound bus in the mid-1920s. Photograph courtesy of the Minnesota Historical Society.

their credit, a mistake that caught up with them in the aftermath of the stock market crash in 1929. As their stock price plummeted, the *Wall Street Journal* described their plight in words echoed often during the latest stock market "correction": "Their financing had stood on the assumption that boom times were normal times." Greyhound's largest stockholder was the Atlas Corporation, which held seventy thousand shares. A financial expert from Atlas met with Glenn Traer, Greyhound's head of finance, to analyze the numbers and assess the company's viability. Traer showed the Atlas expert how the net profit from one complete bus run on a normal day was $4.50. The expert wondered how any company could survive on such a small profit, and Traer agreed—if the company had only one bus run. Greyhound had eighteen hundred runs a day for a daily net profit of $8,100, totaling nearly $3 million in profits annually. Impressed with the company's potential, the Atlas expert worked with Traer to keep Greyhound running during the depression.

Its fortunes turned in 1933 when Greyhound gained exclusive rights to provide transportation within the Chicago "Century of Progress" Exposition. Taking advantage of the opportunity, Greyhound reserved two thousand hotel rooms and advertised bus tours to the exposition from every state in the Union. Transportation within the fair netted a half-million dollars while the bus tours earned millions.

Wickman continued to lead Greyhound until 1946, when he retired at age fifty-nine. One indication of his effectiveness as a leader appears in the company's revenues after his retirement: despite prosperous postwar times, they declined from nearly $20 million to $17 million in 1947, $16 million in 1948, and $11.6 million in 1949. Like many successful entrepreneurs, Wickman started with a small idea to profit from a local need and built up a solid business in the process. Unlike most entrepreneurs, he sold the business even though it was growing and even though he had nothing substantial to take its place. What he did have was the uncommon sense that bus service had much broader potential and that he could neither explore nor exploit that opportunity while he ran a successful business in Hibbing.

In many ways, the enduring enterprise founded by Colonel Lewis Brittin paralleled Wickman's experience at Greyhound. Brittin started small in the Upper Midwest and ended up with a national transportation company. He pushed hard to provide more efficient service to a growing number of communities. Like Wickman, his haste to expand led to decisions that later haunted his company. For all their similarities, however, Wickman and Brittin faced very different obstacles because of the transportation they provided: while Wickman and his drivers worried about frostbite and rough roads, Brittin's pilots worried about falling out of the sky.

Colonel Lewis Brittin

Nine months after Colonel Lewis Brittin established Northwest Airways to make airmail runs to the Twin Cities, he organized its first passenger flight. A small group of people gathered on July 5, 1927, at Speedway Field, an automobile raceway converted into an airport where Minneapolis–St. Paul International Airport now stands. The pilot, known to his friends as Charlie Holman and to his adoring public as "Speed," pulled on his trademark helmet and goggles, which he wore even though the biplane had a closed cockpit.

That same year Holman had entered the National Air Derby, a race from New York City to Spokane, Washington. When he reached Butte, Montana, Holman learned that he was sixteen minutes behind the leader, so he rejected the best-known route through the Rockies in favor of a risky shortcut and won the race by nineteen seconds. A few days later he won a race from Spokane to Portland, Oregon. He received a hero's welcome when he returned home, with parades in his honor in both Minneapolis and St. Paul.

Holman waited patiently as Brittin asked Northwest's first scheduled passenger, the mayor of St. Paul, if he was ready to fly to Chicago. The mayor looked at the plane and its daredevil pilot, hesitated, and then backed out. He had good reason: One year earlier, Charles "Pop" Dickinson had been awarded the Twin Cities–to–Chicago airmail contract. Fifteen minutes after his pilot took off with the first load of mail, a violent summer storm knocked the plane out of the air, killing the pilot. Dickinson got the contract because the Post Office Department had given up trying to provide airmail service on its own after a short, but disastrous, trial. Air Corps reservist Charles Lindbergh, for example, parachuted to safety four times while delivering the

Colonel Lewis Brittin. Photograph by Underwood and Underwood of Chicago. Courtesy of the Minnesota Historical Society.

mail. The Air Corps run from Minneapolis to Chicago lasted just nine months, during which eight planes crashed and four pilots were killed.

After the mayor's understandable change of heart, Brittin scanned the crowd for a replacement. He spotted Byron Webster, a St. Paul executive, and offered to write him the number-one ticket on Northwest Airways. Webster eagerly accepted. The tall, twenty-eight-year-old Holman boosted Webster into the cockpit, then climbed in and took off for Chicago. As they flew over the confluence of the Mississippi and St. Croix Rivers, Webster later recalled, "the engine suddenly went deader than a smelt." Holman calmly landed the plane in a field, hauled out a tool kit, and fixed the engine. Needing to lighten the load to take off from the bumpy farm field, Holman walked to a nearby farmhouse and called Brittin, who sent a truck from St. Paul. The truck took the mail sacks and Webster back to Speedway Field, where Holman met them, and Holman, Webster, and the mail took off once again. The plane stopped in La Crosse, Madison, and Milwaukee, Wisconsin, for mail, arriving in Milwaukee at midnight in almost total darkness. Holman and Webster decided to complete the trip and landed in Chicago at 2:30 A.M. The four-hundred-mile journey had taken more than twelve hours.

Holman's determination reflected that of his boss. Lewis Brittin was orphaned as a child in Connecticut, growing up in boarding schools before passing the entrance exams to both Harvard and Yale. He chose Harvard but ran out of money after his first year, so he worked construction to pay for the industrial engineering degree he earned at night. During World War I he was promoted to the rank of lieutenant colonel in the Quartermaster Corps, and he was called "Colonel" thereafter. Following the war Brittin joined General Electric, which sent him to Minneapolis to work on a project. Local businessmen hired him away from GE to design and build the Northwest Terminal, an industrial district offering the combined facilities of the railroads serving the Twin Cities. His performance impressed several business leaders, who put him in charge of their business-development activities.

During the 1920s, Henry Ford sponsored a traveling air show to demonstrate the practicality of flying. Brittin persuaded Ford to send one of his Ford Reliability Tours to the Twin Cities. He was also instrumental in getting Ford to build the largest Ford auto-assembly plant outside of Detroit in St. Paul, just across the river from Minnehaha Falls.

As director of industrial development for the St. Paul Association (the predecessor of the city's chamber of commerce), Brittin believed aviation was key to the area's growth. When "Pop" Dickinson notified the Post Office Department that he was going out of business on October 1, 1926, Brittin asked a number of individuals and groups to take over the route. They all declined, prompting Brittin to say, "If nobody else will keep this thing alive, then I'll do it myself." He had no money, no planes, no pilots, no airmail contract, and no employees.

He tackled the money issue first, persuading his friends at Ford to arrange a meeting with wealthy Detroiters, twenty-nine of whom chipped in to make Northwest Airways a Michigan corporation with a stock value of $300,000. Returning home, Brittin put his newfound capital to work, hiring ten people, including two pilots, and buying two open-cockpit biplanes. The Post Office Department, which had received no offers for the Twin Cities airmail route, gladly accepted Brittin's bid. He then spearheaded a drive to raise a $295,000 bond issue to build a new airport near downtown St. Paul (now called Holman Field).

The airline lost $900 in its first three months, but Brittin and its owners had expected worse. One hundred and six passengers flew Northwest in 1927 before it suspended service for the winter, an impressive number considering the primitive flying conditions. Pilots flew in almost complete darkness once the sun set, the only visible light being a revolving beacon atop the Milwaukee airport hangar. In bad weather a pilot would circle a farmhouse until the farmer emerged, got out the family car, and drove to a nearby field to illuminate it with the car's headlights.

In 1928 Brittin persuaded four railroads to coordinate their schedules with Northwest for "plane-and-train" travel. Passengers coming from New York to the Midwest could fly for part of the trip (daylight only) and cut eight hours off their journeys. To add credibility to his young airline and his unusual proposal, he hired Charles Lindbergh as a technical adviser. Brittin's flair for publicity, evident in the group he assembled for Northwest's first passenger flight and in the aviation celebrities he involved in his young company—a list that included Speed Holman, Charles Lindbergh, and Amelia Earhart—helped establish Northwest Airways as a legitimate airline.

In 1928 Holman won the Los Angeles to Cincinnati Air Derby, then set a world record by looping-the-loop 1,433 times in five hours over the St. Paul airport that now bears his name. The feat was even more amazing considering that Holman had been guest of honor the night before at a party celebrating his Air Derby victory and had gotten less than an hour of sleep before his dizzying accomplishment. In the fall Holman flew in the National Air Derby between New York and Los Angeles, although he got only as far as Pennsylvania. Flying blind in a dense black fog for hours, he ran out of fuel and had to make a dead-stick landing in a small clearing on the side of a mountain.

Holman's escapades drew attention to Northwest Airways, and Brittin capitalized on it. Knowing that his airline needed airfields to grow, he volunteered Northwest's help to any midwestern town interested in building landing fields or hangars. More than twenty Minnesota communities accepted his offer, including Rochester, Duluth, Faribault, LeSeur, Marshall, Austin, Mankato, Red Wing, Winona, Hastings, Fairmont, Owatonna, Redwood Falls, and Eveleth. Recognizing the assistance they received from Brittin and Northwest, city officials in Bismarck, North Dakota, named their first airport Brittin Field. Continuing to strengthen his airline's position in 1929, he pulled together a group of Twin Cities executives to buy all the Michigan-held stock in Northwest, bringing ownership of the company to Minnesota. Profits hit $20,000 a month until winter, when the airline still lost money. In his haste to expand, Brittin eagerly agreed to extend airmail service to any community with an airfield and a desire for service, often with negative results. He added seven new stops at small towns in Wisconsin and Illinois that cost more to operate than the airline earned in revenues.

In 1929 Northwest moved its operations to the new St. Paul airport. Brittin and Holman regularly inspected the hangar for neatness, making sure every tool was in its proper place. That same year Northwest initiated night airmail runs after the Department of Commerce installed beacons every ten miles between Chicago and the Twin Cities. Northwest pilots flew the route so often and so close to the ground compared with today's jets that they became very familiar with the landscape, knowledge that saved more than one pilot forced to land in a farmer's field because of bad weather or mechanical difficulty.

Their knowledge saved others as well. In 1930, Northwest pilot Max Freeburg spotted a burning railroad trestle over the Chippewa River near Trevina, Wisconsin. He knew from his frequent trips that a Burlington Northern train was due to cross that trestle in minutes, so he raced toward the train, diving at the engineer while flashing his landing lights and dropping his emergency landing flares. The engineer slammed on the brakes, stopping the train just two hundred feet from the burning trestle. All passengers were safe, including Bobby Jones, who was on his way to Minneapolis to play in the U.S. Open golf championship at Interlachen, a tournament he would win as part of his "grand slam" that year.

Not every flying escapade had such a happy ending. In May 1931 Speed Holman attended the two-day Omaha Air Show, winning a special twenty-five-mile race on the first day. On the second day, Holman offered to entertain the crowd with one of his routine crowd-pleasers: climbing to three hundred feet before stalling the plane,

Charles "Speed" Holman watches passengers board a Northwest Airways plane, circa 1929. Photograph by Northwest Airlines. Courtesy of the Minnesota Historical Society.

leveling off at seventy-five feet, then skimming the field at fifty feet before climbing out of the fall. This time, the plane did not climb. The crash killed Holman. At his funeral, more than one hundred thousand people lined the route to the cemetery, the largest funeral ever held in Minnesota at that time.

Although Brittin mourned the loss of his friend, he did not waver from his vision for Northwest, which now included making it a transcontinental airline. Herbert Hoover's postmaster general wanted two air routes across the United States, one central and the other south, and he forced smaller airlines to merge to make this possible. Northwest managed to avoid the merger mandate because it served the less-populated north. Brittin lobbied for a northern route across the country, arguing that northern cities such as Seattle and Spokane, Washington, which first had to fly people and mail south, deserved better service. Federal officials countered with the assertion that northern weather made the route too dangerous.

On January 28, 1933, Brittin boarded a Northwest plane for a "proof of the pudding" flight from St. Paul to Spokane. To focus media attention on the flight he invited Amelia Earhart to join him. They flew to Billings, where they picked up a Montana sheep rancher who claimed to know every pass through the mountains. They failed to realize that mountain passes look different from the air than on the ground, however, so after nearly crashing twice they decided to ignore the rancher and find their own way, landing in Spokane in a blinding snowstorm. Two days later, after the snow stopped, they flew to Seattle before returning to the Twin Cities. The flight and Brittin's persistence in Washington helped establish a northern cross-country route to Seattle in December 1933.

Brittin resigned from Northwest a short time later during an investigation by the Interstate Commerce Commission into how airlines charged for airmail contracts. Upon learning that the ICC was seizing all airline documents, Brittin worried about the notes he had written describing the idiosyncrasies and weaknesses of senators and congressmen. He raced to his attorney's office, where he tore up and threw away the memos and letters he considered most damaging, but the ICC found the discarded sacks, pasted together several of the colonel's papers, and tried him for contempt of the Senate. He was convicted and sentenced to ten days in jail, which he served in February 1934. After leaving Northwest at the age of fifty-seven to keep from tarnishing its image, he remained in the industry as a private consultant and adviser on aviation matters.

Despite having no knowledge of how to run an airline and no resources to begin one, Colonel Lewis Brittin created an enduring enterprise because of the lessons and connections of his past experiences. He had links to the emerging airline industry through the Ford Reliability Tours. He had access to financial support, first through his contacts at Ford and then through his relationships with Twin Cities business leaders. He understood from his efforts to promote the Northwest Terminal and his clients' business activities that effective public relations helped generate public interest. His involvement with railroads through the Northwest Terminal taught him that transportation companies needed many centralized locations for the efficient exchange of passengers and cargo.

All of these life experiences helped Brittin launch Northwest Airways, which later became Northwest Airlines, but they were not enough to build an enduring enterprise. He also capitalized on his experiences through his vision and persistence. He knew the country needed a northern air route and he made the plans, lobbied people, and provided the proof that Northwest should fly that route. Despite frequent setbacks in a hazardous business, he maneuvered the company into a prominent position in its industry.

A few years after Brittin left Northwest, another Minnesota entrepreneur captured the attitude Brittin exemplified, an attitude common among new business owners. "You can't play it safe," Curt Carlson told a friend. "A person can't be too cautious and be an entrepreneur. You just have to jump in. If things don't turn out right, then you make them right by taking another run at it. Entrepreneurs dig holes and climb out."

Curt Carlson

There's a fine line between not playing it safe and acting foolishly, and Curt Carlson made it a point not to be foolish. His remarks about "jumping in" came eighteen months after he had started the Gold Bond Stamp Company, during which time he had continued to sell soap and other products for Procter and Gamble. He worked for Procter and Gamble during the day and devoted his evenings and weekends to persuading grocers to try his trading stamps. It took a year and a half to acquire forty grocery accounts, at which point Carlson felt ready to invest all of his time in the new venture.

A child of the Great Depression, Carlson grew up in a family dependent on the food business. His father was a grocer and sales representative who often worked twelve-hour days, while his mother operated a bakery. Carlson had his first paper route in 1924 at the age of ten. When the Minneapolis Auditorium opened in 1927, Carlson took advantage of a special offer by the *Minneapolis Journal* of one-week newspaper subscriptions for $1 during the national Rotary convention. He went to the auditorium, where he found long lines of delegates waiting to register. Pitching subscriptions to the captive audience with the promise that people back home could read about the convention while it was happening, Carlson made $300. "The experience taught me that there is always a chance to succeed in a big way, if you can only find the right opportunity," he said.

As a teenager, Carlson organized his own network of newspaper carriers. In high school during the early years of the depression, he maintained his newspaper network while working as a bellhop at Farmers and Mechanics bank, a job he got by demonstrating the same fearless ambition that characterized his life. Riding the elevator after being turned down for a job at General Mills, he asked a fellow passenger if he had been at the employment agency upstairs. The man said he had and described two job

Curt Carlson presides at a Gold Bond Stamp annual meeting in the 1950s. Photograph courtesy of the Carlson Companies.

prospects. Carlson asked which one he was pursuing, then immediately headed for the other, which was at Farmers and Mechanics.

Carlson had his eyes on a blue Chevrolet convertible, so when F and M asked him to work past summer vacation, he accepted. His mother informed him that he had to finish high school. He negotiated with his high-school adviser to skip routine classes if he kept up with the work and still graduate with his own class. Carlson got both the car and the diploma. He continued his education at the University of Minnesota, paying the tuition by delivering groceries, stacking cases of soda pop, hustling newspapers, and working other odd jobs. After graduating in 1937 he welcomed the stability of a job with Procter and Gamble, earning $110 a month. He achieved the largest percentage increase in sales after his first year and was rewarded with an engraved gold watch and a $330 bonus. His success made him wonder what he could earn selling for himself.

One day when he and his wife, Arleen, were shopping at the Leader Department Store in downtown Minneapolis, a sales clerk handed Arleen Security Red Stamps with her purchase. Carlson asked how the stamps worked and the clerk explained the concept of filling a book with stamps, then redeeming it for $2 in cash.

Before a man or woman becomes an entrepreneur, an idea often forms around a simple "what if" question. Cadwallader Washburn asked, "What if we found a way to make spring wheat as salable as winter wheat?" James J. Hill wondered, "What if we built a northern route to the Pacific?" Hans Andersen thought, "What if we standardized window sizes?" John Brandt asked, "What if cooperatives sold their products directly to consumers?"

"What if" questions have launched enduring enterprises, pointed them in new directions, and revived waning fortunes. In hindsight the solutions they trigger often seem so commonsense and practical that one wonders why they weren't discovered sooner. In some cases they were, but insights are not successful businesses. A promising idea may arise by asking "what if," but it will not become a promising business unless it is acted upon.

After learning about trading stamps, Curt Carlson asked, "What if grocers used trading stamps to attract and keep customers?" He knew from experience that grocers had a tough time differentiating themselves from the competition because they all carried the same products, which they all sold at roughly the same price. What if they could offer their customers something their competitors did not have? Excited by the idea, Carlson discussed it with his University of Minnesota economics professor, a local banker, his parents, and his wife. They all advised against it; the financial struggles of the depression were too recent to risk the security of a stable job on an unproven idea. Carlson understood the risks, which was why he kept his day job with Procter and Gamble, but he also decided to act on his idea.

First, he needed a name for his stamps. He remembered from a college advertising course that you could choose an unusual or distinctive name if you had a lot of money to promote it—which he didn't—or you could choose a familiar name with positive

Gold Bond Stamp book. Photograph courtesy of the Carlson Companies.

connotations. Carlson liked "gold" because it represented value and "bond" for safety. The Gold Bond Stamp Company began on June 8, 1938.

Like many budding entrepreneurs, he minimized risk by keeping expenses down. He paid someone else's secretary $5 a month to answer the Gold Bond phone. Lacking money for a lawyer, he paid a secretary at the Leader Department Store $5 to show him the store's contract with Security Red Stamp, then copied it and substituted "Gold Bond" for "Security Red." When he needed money to print his first batch of stamps, he asked his landlord if he could pay the $55 rent at the end of the month rather than the beginning, and the landlord agreed.

Success came slowly. Carlson's contract asked for 2 percent of gross sales for the stamp program, a significant amount in a low-margin business. The promise of a 20-percent increase in sales did little to persuade grocers to join the program. It took nine months before he closed his first sale for a stamp order of $14.50.

Curt Carlson believed in goals. The first goal for his new business was to make $100 a week. He wrote the goal on a slip of paper and kept it in his wallet, removing it frequently to assess his progress. When he reached that goal, he put another in his wallet. By 1942 he was setting five-year goals. He also didn't believe in playing it safe, and near the end of 1939 he left Procter and Gamble to work full-time on Gold Bond stamps. Reflecting on the knowledge he gained while at Procter and Gamble, Carlson wrote in his autobiography that, "with the benefit of both experience and hindsight, I would strongly urge every young man or woman with entrepreneurial stirrings to do what I did: spend some time learning from an already successful enterprise what the business world is all about."

Carlson faced a cash-flow problem in 1939 when he had to pay for stamp promotions at stores new to the program before getting any money from them. He asked a bank for a $1,000 loan but was declined, even though he had signed contracts in hand. Eventually he had to sell a half-dozen $100 shares in his company to friends, which he bought back as soon as possible.

By 1941 he had two hundred grocery accounts in the Twin Cities; three months after the Japanese bombed Pearl Harbor he had fewer than seventy. Food shortages during the war allowed grocers to sell whatever they stocked, eliminating the need for Gold Bond stamps. Carlson stayed in business by taking a job as sales manager for his father-in-law's clothing store. Waiting for a draft notice that never came, he persuaded a Procter and Gamble executive to become his partner and run the business if Carlson could not.

After the war the two men opened up new territories and expanded the stamp business to service stations, dry cleaners, and other stores. The promise of a 20-percent increase in sales became a fact they could prove through data they had collected from stores that carried Gold Bond stamps.

Carlson had a five-year plan that focused on selling to grocery chains, but it took seven years before the plan became a reality. In April 1953 Supervalu stores in Minneapolis began offering Gold Bond stamps. Instead of cash for the redeemed stamps, customers selected merchandise from a catalog. The company heavily promoted the concept, advertising by mail, radio, and newspaper, and the stores were jammed. Supervalu's sales jumped 63 percent in the first nine months.

The Supervalu account transformed the Gold Bond Stamp Company. Before Supervalu, Carlson's typical Gold Bond account used ten pads of stamps a month, a sale of about $145. Supervalu's first check to Carlson was for $250,000. It required Carlson's company to have warehouses and inventory, merchandising expertise, redemption centers, catalogs, office space, and a lot more employees. "Every entrepreneur, at some point in his company's development, reaches a watershed, after which the way he does business is dramatically and forever changed," Carlson observed in his autobiography.

Supervalu's success motivated food-chain giant Kroger to contact Carlson about its own stamp program. When Supervalu objected to the use of Gold Bond stamps, Carlson created the Top Value stamp program for Kroger, which it purchased from him in 1957 for $1 million. At that point, he bought out his partner for a lump sum of $1 million and $50,000 a year for five years.

During the next few years Carlson expanded into California and Canada, the Caribbean, Japan, and other countries, but his trading-stamp business was peaking. It had ballooned from twenty-three billion stamps worth $50 million in 1952 to twenty times that in 1968. However, in the early 1960s Americans became more interested in discounts than premiums and they blamed trading stamps for higher prices. Carlson bucked the trend before deciding to change his business through diversification and acquisition, moving into hotels and real estate first, then restaurants, catalog showrooms, manufacturing, and other industries as he built Carlson Companies.

He knew real estate because of the experience gained operating 330 Gold Bond Gift Centers and nine warehouses. He bought the flagging Radisson Hotel in downtown Minneapolis, intent on turning it around through his promotional savvy, then built a chain of Radisson Hotels in line with his replication strategy, a strategy he also applied to such Carlson acquisitions as T.G.I. Friday and Country Kitchen restaurants and Ask Mr. Foster travel agencies. The strategy worked; annual revenue topped $1 billion in 1977, $2 billion in 1982, and $3 billion in 1985.

Although nearly all entrepreneurs featured in this book overcame adversity to create enduring enterprises, none exhibited more tenacity than those who founded businesses shortly before or during the Great Depression as corporations went bankrupt, people lost their jobs, credit dried up, and banks failed. An estimated twenty-five million stockholders were wiped out in the last two months of 1929. During the next four years, approximately one hundred thousand people lost their jobs every week.

In 1931, 61 percent of the manufacturing companies in Minnesota reported operating losses. The next year that number climbed to 86 percent. By 1932, 70 percent of the miners on the Iron Range had lost their jobs. By 1934, one-third of working people in Hennepin County were unemployed. All industries were affected, but Minnesota's food industries suffered less than metals, machinery, and paper, helping to buffer the state's economy from the worst of the depression. The country did not begin to recover until 1936 and had still not regained its form when World War II demanded even more sacrifice.

The entrepreneurs of this era demonstrated that unwavering persistence in the pursuit of a dream rarely fails. As Curt Carlson once said, "Whatever you do, do with integrity. Wherever you go, go as a leader. Whomever you serve, serve with caring. Whenever you dream, dream with your all. And never, ever give up."

Building on Talent (1940–1965)

Sister Elizabeth Kenny

The entrepreneur who may best exemplify Curt Carlson's advice to "never, ever give up" came to Minnesota late in her life, having served as a nurse during World War I before fighting her own decades-long battle against the medical establishment. While she had started several hospitals and clinics in her native land, she was sixty-one years old when her Minneapolis clinic opened, affirming the timeless value of a good idea.

Sister Elizabeth Kenny came to Minneapolis from Australia in 1940 at the age of fifty-nine. A controversial advocate of a radical treatment for poliomyelitis, she arrived in a year that saw nearly ten thousand Minnesotans contract the polio virus. Six years later Minneapolis alone would count that many cases. Parents feared exposing their children to a virus so common that even the president of the United States had not escaped it.

Franklin Roosevelt, who used a wheelchair because of the disease, helped launch the March of Dimes to combat polio, and the crusade supported a national priority. Dimes grew into dollars until millions had been raised for the cause, money that eventually eradicated polio by helping fund the development of the Salk and Sabin vaccines in the mid-1950s. Before the arrival of the vaccine, however, physicians could treat only the effects of the infectious disease, which damages motor nerve cells in the spinal cord. Muscle paralysis can occur within days of the first symptoms. The popular name for the disease, infantile paralysis, reflects its most common victims, children under five years of age, although older children and adults were also at risk. Roosevelt contracted polio at the age of thirty-nine.

Doctors believed that the virus caused irretrievable paralysis because strong, healthy

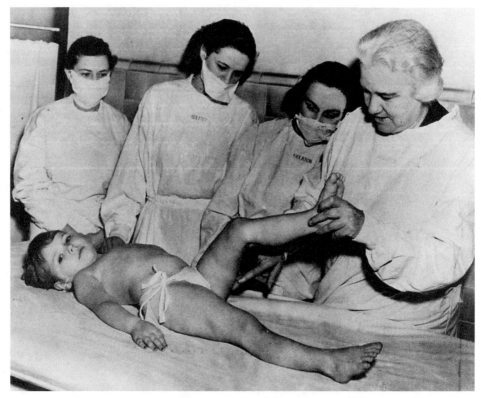

Sister Elizabeth Kenny demonstrates her therapy techniques at her clinic in Minneapolis.
Photograph courtesy of the Minnesota Historical Society.

muscles pulled on weakened ones. The prescribed treatment involved rigid splinting
to immobilize the affected muscles. Although the approach led to atrophied muscles
and lifelong paralysis, the worldwide medical community believed it offered the only
hope for recovery. Sister Kenny stood against this practice and the doctors who supported it, and she often stood alone. In 1911 she had successfully treated the first six
cases of polio she had encountered, and her experience told her the doctors were
wrong. For much of the next three decades she fought the arrogance, ignorance, and
skepticism of the medical establishment to promote her unorthodox approach, armed
with an unwavering belief in the superiority of her treatment and an unending desire
to help polio victims lead more normal lives.

Liza Kenny was born in 1880 in the Australian village of Warialda. She was 75 percent
Irish and 25 percent Scottish—"for some balance," she liked to say. She first learned
about muscles at the age of eighteen when her local doctor lent her a textbook so that
she could help her frail eleven-year-old brother get stronger. She learned well: her
brother developed into a stellar athlete. When Kenny decided to become a missionary and was told that a missionary should also be a nurse, she acquired nursing skills
and experience by working for doctors. When one of the doctors gave her a letter de-

scribing the satisfactory work she had done, she felt she had all the qualifications she needed, had a nurse's outfit made, and became a self-appointed bush nurse.

Kenny rode her horse to isolated settlements and ranches, delivering babies, treating injuries and illnesses, and learning medicine. In June 1911 she cared for a two-year-old girl who was unable to move. Kenny had not seen such paralysis before, and, unsure how to proceed, rode several miles to the nearest telegraph office to wire the local doctor for advice. Several hours later she got a reply: it sounded like infantile paralysis, there was no known treatment, and she should do the best she could. Returning to the house she found the girl in immense pain from her twisted leg. Kenny thought the girl's leg muscles looked shortened and tightened, "in spasm," and decided she must first relieve the contractions. She found that strips of wool soaked in boiling water eased the tension.

Within a few days six of twenty children in the area had contracted polio. She treated each child the same way, relieving the contractions with moist heat, then helping each child learn how to use the affected limbs again, moving them gently, patiently, while softly encouraging the children to remember how their legs and arms worked. Their strength gradually returned until they were once again running and playing.

When she later met with the doctor who had advised her, she described what she had done and told him the patients had fully recovered. He did not believe her and asked her to demonstrate her treatment on a boy stricken by polio and in pain from the splints that immobilized both his legs. She removed the splints, covered his legs with strips of a blanket soaked in hot water, and explained how she worked the muscles once the pain was gone. Still skeptical, the doctor told her that her treatment contradicted accepted practice and warned her not to fight the medical profession because it did not tolerate reformers. While he encouraged Kenny to proceed with her ideas, he did not adopt the new methods himself, nor did he take her to the local hospital to treat other polio patients.

For the next ten years Liza Kenny practiced nursing, first in a hospital she opened in an empty house, then as a member of the Australian Army Nursing Service during World War I. She served mainly on troopships carrying wounded soldiers from Europe to Australia, traveling nearly two hundred thousand miles during the war.

Near the end of 1918 she became ill, was diagnosed with an inflammation of the muscular wall of the heart, and told she had six months to live. Unable to rest, Kenny ran a temporary isolation hospital for flu victims until the epidemic that would kill twenty million people worldwide subsided. She returned home only to have her doctor confirm the previous diagnosis and set her life expectancy at four months. She got out of bed, got dressed, and sailed for Dublin to consult specialists there. Four months passed with a slight improvement in her condition and she returned to Australia. While she recovered she resumed bush nursing. The people she served affectionately referred to her as "sister" and the title stuck. Although she belonged to no religious order and had no nursing degree, Sister Kenny provided expert medical care through a rare blend of common sense, courage, creativity, and confidence.

In May 1926 the sister of a friend fell off the back of a plow, breaking her left thigh and right ankle and severing two toes. Based on her experience, Kenny didn't think the girl could survive a thirty-mile ambulance ride over rutted roads. She had a wooden cupboard door removed and laid the girl upon it, then tied her to the door with strips of sheeting and tucked hot water bottles around her to reduce the shock. The girl survived the trip. Sister Kenny modified and patented her stretcher, which was eventually sold worldwide.

In 1933 four Australian doctors wrote a letter to the health minister encouraging the government to train special polio therapists under Sister Kenny's direction. She demonstrated her techniques to medical experts in Brisbane, one of whom characterized her as "a seemingly ignorant, uncouth bush nurse." She antagonized the doctors with sharp criticism of accepted practice and an unshakable belief in her own approach. While a few offered support, most dismissed her techniques as unscientific and unproven. But the prevailing opinion did not stop Sister Kenny, and she opened the Sister Kenny Clinic and Training School in Brisbane in 1934. Two years later she and her staff of three medical officers and forty-eight assistants had more than six hundred patients in four Australian cities.

Her doctors and nurses joined the army when World War II started. Frustrated by the lack of support and assistance, Kenny welcomed the suggestion of a doctor who had just returned from Mayo Clinic that she share her techniques with its specialists. After stops in Denver, New York, and Chicago, Kenny and her adopted daughter, Mary, arrived in Rochester, Minnesota, in May 1940. The few doctors she met could not believe that her unorthodox treatment worked, but their skepticism was tempered by the positive reports from Australia. They recommended that she go to the Twin Cities because it had far more polio cases following an outbreak the previous year. For three days Kenny demonstrated her treatment at three Twin Cities hospitals. A few days later one of the doctors, convinced of the merit in her approach, ordered all the frames, splints, and casts removed from his polio cases at Gillette and St. Paul Children's hospitals. Wallace Cole, chief of orthopedics at the University of Minnesota medical school, asked her what she would need to stay in Minnesota. "A bed and a meal a day," she replied.

As in her native land, the conversion of a few doctors was overshadowed by the skepticism of most. John Pohl, a thirty-six-year-old attending orthopedist at Abbott Hospital in Minneapolis, doubted that Kenny's approach worked, but he was willing to try anything that might relieve the agony of children in casts. He introduced her to an eighteen-year-old patient, Henry Haverstock, who had contracted polio in 1939. After five months of the approved treatment he had received four months of physiotherapy, yet he still had a curved spine, paralyzed right leg, nearly useless left leg, one weak arm, and weak chest, back, and abdominal muscles. Fitted with steel leg braces, an arm splint, and a steel-and-canvas body corset, he was told he would never walk again. Sister Kenny removed his braces. She used heat and gentle movement to relieve the pain and helped him learn how to use his muscles again. Within a week he could straighten one of his legs. By the end of the year he could walk with a pair of hand crutches. In the spring of 1942 he enrolled in the University of Minnesota, from which he graduated and became a practicing attorney.

The case converted Pohl to the Kenny method. He convinced the Minneapolis Board of Public Welfare to give her space and equipment at Minneapolis General Hospital. In 1941 she began teaching her approach to students at the U of M. The August 1941 issue of *American Weekly*, distributed to millions of American homes in the Sunday newspaper, reported that "a new and revolutionary treatment for infantile paralysis is now being tested and demonstrated." Four months later a national polio foundation stated that "the length of time during which pain, tenderness, and spasm are present is greatly reduced, and contractures caused by muscle shortening . . . are prevented by the Kenny method." The American Medical Association concurred. Asked if she was excited by the validation of her work, Kenny said she was gratified, but that the time had passed "when I could feel any emotion over the publication of a fact that had been evident to me for almost half a lifetime."

Almost overnight doctors and nurses across the country switched from splinting and inactivity to heat and activity. The U of M offered courses in the Kenny method with funding from the March of Dimes. When it couldn't meet the demand, it established five training centers across the country. The need for therapists produced a growing number of people who had received only a minimal amount of instruction. Sister Kenny lobbied the city of Minneapolis for a place where she could provide more thorough training, and the city agreed. The Sister Kenny Institute opened in a building on Eighteenth Street and Chicago Avenue in December 1942.

That same year, the *New York Sun* named Sister Kenny its outstanding woman of the year. Four years later Hollywood released a movie about her life starring Rosalind Russell. In 1943 the Gallup Poll ranked her just behind Eleanor Roosevelt as the woman American women admired most; Kenny would remain on the list for nine consecutive years. In 1952, a year before she died, she surpassed Roosevelt as the most admired woman in the country.

Despite the accolades, controversy about the nature of the polio virus and the effectiveness of her treatments continued to plague Sister Kenny. Brash and unapologetic, she irritated those who questioned her methods by proclaiming the rightness of her cause. "I am correct and the rest of the world is wrong. I cannot deny what my eyes see," she said. "I am engaged in a terrible struggle. I have to have the bulldog courage to hear the cries of the afflicted children."

Although vaccine effectively ended those cries shortly after Kenny's death, her institute evolved into one of the world's most respected rehabilitation centers, dedicated to patient care, research, and education. Not only did she launch an organization that succeeded beyond belief, she revolutionized medical attitudes about the value of activity over immobilization. That Elizabeth Kenny accomplished this on

Sister Kenny and her daughter, Mary, are met by Cary Grant at the opening of the movie *Sister Kenny* in 1946. Photograph courtesy of the Minnesota Historical Society.

The Sister Kenny Institute opened in Minneapolis in December 1942. Photograph courtesy of the Minnesota Historical Society.

an international stage without a medical degree, scientific support, or institutional backing affirms the power one individual has to inspire change. As Goethe wrote, "Boldness has genius, power, and magic in it."

Sister Kenny arrived in Minnesota at a turning point for business in the state. World War II drew heavily on the state's resources, and that demand transformed the commercial landscape. The Iron Range supplied nearly 70 percent of the nation's iron ore during the war, depleting its supply of high-grade ore. In 1946 Reserve Mining began construction of the state's first taconite plant to process the low-grade ore that remained.

While the iron mines were surpassing all previous levels of production, Minnesota's farmers produced record crops. General Mills and Pillsbury made huge quantities of flour and other products while Pillsbury invented a sack that protected food dropped into the ocean for waiting soldiers.

The number of manufacturing employees in the state grew from ninety-five thousand in 1939 to one hundred ninety-five thousand in 1947 as companies contributed to the war effort. 3M made window tape for bomb raids and sheeting for airplane wings. Mayo Clinic helped pilots stay conscious during rapid acceleration by assisting with the development of the G suit. Andersen Corporation made prefabricated huts for Army Air Corps bases. Honeywell designed an autopilot that allowed pilots to bail out before their planes crashed, saving up to one thousand lives. Northern Pump made gun mounts. Minneapolis Moline produced artillery shells. Crown Auto Works built portable bridges. International Harvester made aircraft guns. Munsingwear provided large quantities of underwear for American soldiers. North Star Woolen Mills and Faribo Mills made blankets for the Allies.

Shortly after the war ended, so did agriculture's reign over Minnesota's economy. By 1950, for the first time in the state's history, more Minnesotans lived in urban areas than in rural towns and on farms. By 1958 the value of manufacturing in the state had surpassed the value of farming by more than $500 million. Postwar families unable to find housing in the inner cities moved to the suburbs. Spending grew on the family car. Legislators appropriated funds to construct a grid of highways that would make commuting more convenient. To serve the growing numbers of suburban shoppers, Dayton's announced plans to build a $10 million shopping center in Edina. Southdale, the world's first fully enclosed regional mall, opened in 1956.

The millions of government dollars spent during the war on producing goods and developing technologies helped release all the energy the long depression had restrained. Research in science and engineering in the war years led to technological advances in manufacturing, which contributed to Minnesota's emergence as an electronics leader in the 1950s. By 1960 the state had 117 companies in electronics and related industries that made a variety of products, including tape recorders, electronic circuits, hearing aids, radar indicators, conveyor systems, biomedical instruments, radio and television sets, thermostats, and copying machines.

The GI bill helped returning soldiers finance their college educations, and many chose careers in engineering. Others learned new technologies and skills during their military service that became the impetus for new enterprises when they returned to civilian life. Such was the case for William Norris.

William Norris

During World War II William Norris served in the Naval Reserve as a code breaker. His ability to break down a complex problem, interpret the parts individually, understand how they were related, then solve the problem helped his group develop speedier code-breaking devices.

When the war ended, a colleague suggested that Norris and others in his group start a company to continue their work, with the promise that the navy would send contracts their way. An uncertain postwar economy and the lack of venture capital limited their financing options to willing investors, which they found in John Parker, an investment banker and Annapolis graduate.

Norris and his colleagues invested $10,000 in the new company, as did Parker, who also established a $200,000 credit line. Their company, Engineering Research Associates, began in St. Paul in 1946, housed in an empty building Parker had used to make wooden gliders during the war. Parker was president of the company and Norris vice president of marketing. Within a year Parker put Norris in charge of all St. Paul operations.

By 1950 ERA had become a leader in designing and building computers. The technology they developed for government applications delivered advanced electronic data processing and storage, putting ERA in prime position at the dawn of the computer age. John Parker figured his company needed $5 million to $10 million to become a leader in the computer business. Lacking such capital, he decided to sell the company to Remington Rand, which had built the world's first business computer in 1949, for Rand stock worth $1.7 million, realizing a sizable return on ERA's $20,000 start-up cost.

Norris knew nothing about the sale and adamantly opposed it when he was informed. "We had enormous technology and we were much more advanced than any other company," he later said. "IBM at that time was still a small outfit and didn't have the advanced knowledge we had in ERA. It was the chance of a lifetime, and we missed it when Johnny Parker sold out to Jim Rand." While ERA represented an investment to Parker, it was a passion for Norris and his engineers. During the next five years ERA became a major computer supplier to the armed forces, but it lost ground to IBM in the commercial market. A risk-averse Remington Rand had failed to take advantage of a rare opportunity.

In 1955 Rand merged with Sperry and consolidated its computer business in St. Paul under the Univac name, with Norris in charge. He warned Sperry Rand's CEO that he couldn't make the company number one in computers and be profitable in the short term. The CEO told Norris not to worry, because he wanted Univac to be another IBM and he had the resources to do it. Unfortunately for Norris, the CEO did not understand what resources would be required. When the company realized that

William Norris. Photograph courtesy of the Charles Babbage Institute, University of Minnesota.

the cost of competing in the computer market was hundreds of millions of dollars, it denied appropriations to Univac, killed programs, and narrowed Norris's responsibilities. Faced with a choice between biding time while he climbed the corporate ladder or exercising his entrepreneurial talent, Norris chose to set out on his own, motivated in part by the words of Sperry Rand's famous board chair, General Douglas MacArthur.

MacArthur attended meetings at the company's Connecticut headquarters every Thursday. When Norris had corporate business at headquarters, he made it a point to show up on Thursdays. He frequently rode back to New York with MacArthur, and during these trips he would learn from the general's colorful military experiences. One MacArthur maxim became a Norris motto: "There is no such thing as security in this world. There is only opportunity."

Norris seized his opportunity. He and eleven talented Univac engineers left Sperry Rand in 1957 to form a new company they named Control Data. Their first order of business was to sell stock in a company that had no products, no other employees, and no facilities. Investors recognized the value of Control Data's founders, however, and within two weeks had bought 615,000 shares at a dollar each. Norris himself mortgaged nearly everything he owned to buy 75,000 shares. With the stock as collateral the company secured bank loans equal to four times their investment.

One Sperry engineer who followed Norris was thirty-one-year-old Seymour Cray, a computer genius who hated distractions, often arriving at work at noon and remaining well into the night. He preferred working alone or with a few engineers and loathed bureaucracy and details. An indication of his disdain for anything corporate was an early business plan he submitted to Norris. After stalling for as long as possible, Cray finally acquiesced with one of the shortest and most ambitious plans ever written: "Five-year goal: Build the biggest computer in the world. One-year goal: Achieve one-fifth of above."

Although some leaders of the new company wanted to pursue the commercial computer market, Cray convinced Norris of the value of building big computers. Realizing that Control Data could not remain small and compete with IBM and others, Norris began acquiring companies just four months after his company started. His acquisitions accelerated in the mid-1960s when Control Data bought twenty-five companies in just four years, gaining the technology, human resources, and facilities it needed to compete.

Control Data introduced the world's most powerful computer in 1960. The 1604, designed by Cray, was compact and versatile at half the cost of a comparable IBM computer. It was one of the first computers to replace vacuum tubes with transistors, which Cray bought at a local electronics store to save money. He also designed Control Data's next two products, a desk-sized computer and the CDC 6600, the largest computer ever built at that time.

Big computers proved profitable for Control Data as sales jumped from $4.5 million in 1959 to $28 million the next year, $100 million in 1963, and $1 billion in 1969. IBM resented the fact that Control Data was siphoning off the top end of its business and responded first by modifying an existing computer and selling it for much less than the 1604, then countering every Control Data move by offering new upgrades and more power or the promise of a comparable IBM system. When Control Data announced the introduction of the CDC 6600, the world's first supercomputer, IBM announced it was developing a computer that would dwarf the 6600. It never delivered on its promise, but the announcement alone kept customers from buying from Control Data, nearly bankrupting the company.

By 1968 Norris had seen and documented enough monopolistic practices to sue IBM. Many of his staff members argued against taking on the industry giant but Norris persisted, betting the company on a lawsuit that escalated into one of the largest and most complex antitrust cases in history. The parties settled out of court in 1973 with Control Data receiving $100 million both from IBM and its Service Bureau Corporation.

The competition with IBM figured into Norris's decision to expand the company's business. His supercomputers needed peripherals, such as disk drives and controllers, that Control Data did not make. The only supplier in some cases was IBM, which charged more than Norris was willing to pay. He learned that Control Data could make its own peripherals, but to do so economically it had to produce more than it could use. Norris decided to enter the peripherals manufacturing business and sell to other manufacturers. Ironically, Control Data eventually manufactured IBM-compatible disk drives and controllers priced lower than IBM's own peripherals.

Early Control Data computers competed with IBM in the large-computer market. Photograph courtesy of the Minnesota Historical Society.

The decisions to sue IBM and make peripherals exemplified the aggressive, risk-taking nature of William Norris. He liked to say, "Whenever I see everybody going south, I have a great compulsion to go north." Being contrary had served him well from a young age. In 1932, shortly after the death of his father, he graduated from the University of Nebraska, then returned to the family farm to help his mother survive the drought that had turned the Great Plains into a dust bowl.

His immediate problem was feeding the cattle during the coming winter. Norris had observed that cattle often ate Russian thistle even when they could graze on alfalfa. With an abundant supply of the tumbleweed readily available, he decided to harvest it and feed it to his cattle all winter. Local farmers, most of whom sold their cattle before winter because of the lack of feed, thought he was crazy. He couldn't get them to help him bring in the thistle because they didn't want to look foolish. The next spring the neighbors were surprised to find the Norris cattle thinner but alive and bearing healthy calves. Research would later prove the thistle high in protein.

William Norris applied his contrary nature, willingness to take risks, and ability to grasp complex issues to the growth of Control Data, making it the world's fourth-largest computer manufacturer by the mid-1960s. He recognized that the market for supercomputers was limited and introduced time-sharing, which allowed engineering and scientific firms to buy time on CDC computers without having to buy their own. He realized that computer hardware was becoming a commodity business and led the development of proprietary software and technical expertise to differentiate Control Data from its competitors.

Norris believed that a corporation had a social responsibility and, true to his history, took unconventional action. During the nation's urban riots of 1967 he formed a task force to study the issue of minority hiring. The task force recommended putting a manufacturing plant in the inner city. Norris liked the idea and built a facility in a St. Paul minority community, then arranged for all of the company's controllers to be made in this plant, ensuring that the facility would succeed. It did, and the company added inner-city plants in Washington, D.C.; San Antonio, Texas; and Toledo, Ohio.

In 1967 the company's chief financial officer determined that Control Data would need $1 billion over the next ten years to cover the cost of equipment leased to customers, far more than the company could handle. Norris searched for a leasing company to acquire and found Commercial Credit Company, which Control Data acquired even though CCC had ten times Control Data's assets and more than three times its annual earnings. Commercial Credit proved to be a wise decision as it helped Control Data weather downturns in the computer industry.

When Intel released the world's first microprocessor in 1971, the shift from main-frames to personal computers had begun. The next year Seymour Cray left to form his own company when Norris pulled the plug on Cray's new supercomputer to support another designer's project. Norris promoted time-sharing by establishing sixteen computer service centers worldwide. He also opened fifty business and technology centers to provide computer-based training. The centers were linked to a central computer through PLATO, an advanced computer-based instruction system developed by

Control Data. PLATO lost enough money over a long enough period to cause executives to advise Norris to drop it and focus on the company's core business, but Norris believed the company would have eight hundred learning centers by 1985. The proliferation of personal computers dashed his dream. Norris retired from Control Data in 1986.

Norris was not the first to be fooled by the market for computers. Thomas Watson, CEO of IBM, once said, "I think there is a world market for maybe five computers." Kenneth Olson, one of Norris's contemporaries and president and founder of Digital Equipment Corporation, said in 1977, "There is no reason anyone would want a computer in their home." Norris acknowledged smaller businesses' need for computing power by offering time-sharing, but he failed to recognize the full impact of the personal computer. By the mid-1980s Control Data's products were dated and uncompetitive.

Despite the reversal of fortune Control Data evolved into an enduring enterprise, eventually splitting into two companies: Control Data Systems, which develops e-commerce applications, and Ceridian, an information-services company. Norris and his company also helped make Minnesota a leader in the medical-device industry. The computer business trained engineers and technicians, several of whom then applied their knowledge to medical technology. Many of the engineers earned their degrees from the University of Minnesota, and the University Hospitals and medical school encouraged technological solutions to long-standing health problems. When, in the early 1960s, venture capital emerged as a way to finance promising businesses, Minnesota had the ingredients a medical-device company would need to succeed, including the entrepreneur who would pull them all together: Earl Bakken.

Earl Bakken

When he was seventeen years old, Earl Bakken modified a radio and connected it to his high school's public-address system so that students could hear President Franklin Roosevelt ask Congress to declare war on Japan. Such ingenuity would resurface in Bakken's founding of Medtronic and the invention of a battery-powered pacemaker.

As a child growing up in northeast Minneapolis, Bakken was fascinated by electricity. He built a "shock machine" and several radios, set up a private telephone to a friend's home, designed a lighted scoreboard for the high-school football field, and invented a five-foot-tall robot out of Erector-set pieces and plywood. The robot's red eyes blinked and moved up and down while it smoked a cigarette. His mother nurtured his interest by finding vacuum tubes, wires, and switches for his experiments and by agreeing to help her son test his "shock machine." His father stirred young Bakken's imagination by handing down the *Popular Mechanics* magazines he had read. However, nothing inspired the boy as much as the movie monster Frankenstein. The idea that electricity could bring a person back to life became the impetus for a lifelong passion to develop lifesaving medical devices.

This driving force is evident in Bakken's life as early as his college years. After returning from service as an army radar instructor during World War II, he earned bachelor's and master's engineering degrees from the University of Minnesota. In his autobiography, *One Man's Full Life*, he remembers his early medical exposure. "During my spare time," he wrote, "I used to wander across Washington Avenue to the University Hospitals, where I became acquainted with some of the people in their extensive labs and began providing, at their request, an ad-hoc, on-the-spot repair service for malfunctioning equipment." He also got to know physicians and technicians at Northwestern Hospital while waiting for his wife, who worked there as a medical technologist, to finish her shift. They knew Bakken was studying electrical engineering, and when their equipment broke, they asked him to look at it. "It was a win-win situation. They were grateful, and I'd learn something about the machine," Bakken wrote. "I didn't realize it at the time, but I had stumbled onto a career."

Earl Bakken holds an implantable pacemaker in front of a Medtronic "clean room," 1968. Copyright 2002 Star Tribune/Minneapolis–St. Paul. Used by permission.

In the late 1940s, hospital engineers fixed heavy equipment like elevators, not delicate medical instruments. When a piece of equipment broke, it could be taken to a local radio shop for repair or returned to the manufacturer. The first option risked the equipment's performance by trusting it to people who were not trained to fix medical instruments, while the second option risked doing without the equipment for weeks or months until the manufacturer returned it.

Bakken described the situation to his brother-in-law, Palmer Hermundslie, at a family birthday party. The more they talked, the more excited they got about the opportunity, until they agreed to start their own business. They combined the words "medical" and "electronic" to create their new company's name: Medtronic. The year was 1949, more than a decade before venture capital would be available to fund promising start-ups. The men worked out of a railroad boxcar that had been modified and expanded for rebuilding cars. Although the boxcar garage offered little comfort during cold winters or hot summers, it served as Medtronic's "headquarters" for twelve years.

The company earned $8 in its first month. By 1950 Bakken and Hermundslie were augmenting their income from repairs by selling medical equipment for other companies. The manufacturer's representative work not only kept them in business, it enabled them to meet the doctors, nurses, and technicians who would provide information and support when Medtronic eventually entered the pacemaker market.

As with many of the entrepreneurs featured in this book, Bakken learned what he needed to keep his business afloat, unaware of the future value of that knowledge. He made connections with people who would become key customers and advisers, unaware of the critical role they would play in his enduring enterprise. "It would be fun to say that Palmer and I were visionaries who saw the brave new world of sophisticated medical technology spread out in front of us," Bakken wrote in his autobiography. "In truth, however, we didn't see ourselves on the cutting edge of anything."

Even the invention of a battery-powered pacemaker did not inspire dreams of industry leadership. By 1957 Bakken and his small staff of engineers had designed a host of medical devices in response to customer requests: insulated forceps, blood-gas shakers, defibrillators, animal respirators, and cardiac-rate monitors, to name a few. One of his customers, University of Minnesota cardiac surgeon C. Walton Lillehei, asked Bakken to develop a pacemaker with a battery that would help keep babies with congenital heart problems alive while they recovered from surgery. Lillehei and his colleagues had modified large external pacemakers for this purpose, but the equipment relied on AC current for power. Lillehei worried about interruptions in that power. His worst fears were realized on Halloween in 1957: a three-hour blackout claimed the life of an infant who could not survive without a pacemaker. The next day Lillehei pushed Bakken to invent something better.

Contemplating the rhythmic pulse of the heart, Bakken remembered a metronome circuit design he had seen in a *Popular Electronics* magazine. He modified the circuit to produce the right voltages for the heart and added two terminals to create a four-inch-square, inch-and-a-half-thick metal box free of any cords or AC connections. Wires connected to the terminals passed through the patient's chest wall to the heart. When pacing was no longer needed, the wires were removed without reopening the chest.

After a month of development, Bakken brought the device to the university's animal lab for testing. It worked. The next day, when he returned to the hospital on another matter, he happened to walk by the recovery room and notice one of Lillehei's patients wearing his device. Stunned, Bakken found the doctor and asked him for an explanation. "In his typically calm, measured, no-nonsense fashion, he explained that he'd been told by the lab the pacemaker worked, and he didn't want to waste another minute without it," Bakken later wrote. "He said he wouldn't allow a child to die because we hadn't used the best technology available." Lillehei wrote about the new device and demand grew. A year later Medtronic had orders for sixty pacemakers, but it remained just one of many products the company offered.

In upstate New York, Wilson Greatbatch, an electrical engineer, and William Chardack, chief of surgical services at the Veterans Administration hospital in Buffalo, used bipolar electrodes developed by a doctor and a Medtronic electrical engineer to successfully implant a self-contained pacemaker with its own power supply. Palmer Hermundslie flew to Buffalo in October 1960 to sign a contract with Greatbatch and Chardack that gave Medtronic exclusive rights to the implantable pacemaker. Bakken agreed to give Greatbatch and Chardack complete control over every drawing and design change and over communication to the medical community for ten years. Production began a month later in the Twin Cities. By the end of the year, Medtronic had fifty orders at $375 each.

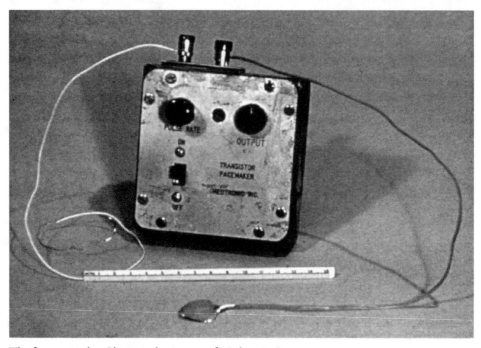

The first pacemaker. Photograph courtesy of Medtronic, Inc.

Sales jumped from $180,000 in 1960 to $518,000 in 1962. Medtronic moved into a new building in northeast Minneapolis to accommodate increased production and a growing number of employees. The company expanded its product line to include a heart-monitoring device and other cardiac devices, which it sold through fourteen salespeople in the United States and Canada and through the tireless efforts of Bakken and Hermundslie. The two leaders traveled extensively, calling on customers and working trade shows. "We were learning that the key to success, by whatever means you wish to measure it, is not to build something and then hope someone will buy it, but to discover what the customer really needs and wants, then to meet or exceed the customer's expectations with both product and service," Bakken wrote.

They also learned about the danger in growing too fast. The new facility, research and development costs, production expenses, expanded staff, trade-show presentations, and customer training sapped Medtronic's limited resources. Bakken had never been too concerned about profits or long-range planning, nor had he given much thought to what kind of company Medtronic should be. Like many entrepreneurs, he worried about what was in front of him and let tomorrow take care of itself.

With Medtronic close to insolvency, Bakken and Hermundslie received an offer from Mallory, the company that supplied its batteries, to buy them out. While they thought it over, Mallory investigated the worldwide market for pacemakers. Its research suggested a potential need for ten thousand devices *total,* a ludicrous claim as erroneous as the computer predictions made by Thomas Watson and Kenneth Olson. Today, five hundred thousand pacemakers are sold *annually.*

Ironically, the number that discouraged Mallory inspired Medtronic. For a company looking at orders in the hundreds, the promise of ten thousand units was astonishing. In 1962, Bakken and Hermundslie secured the financing they needed for their company to grow. The business executives financing Medtronic insisted that Bakken decide what he wanted Medtronic to become, then focus on achieving that goal.

With the counsel of his board of directors, Bakken produced a mission statement that focused on restoring people to "full life." The statement's first tenet clearly captures Medtronic's mission: "to contribute to human welfare by application of biomedical engineering in the research, design, manufacture, and sale of instruments or appliances that alleviate pain, restore health, and extend life." A few years later the company adopted a summary of that statement, "Toward Full Life," that is inscribed on the medallion new Medtronic employees continue to receive today. Forty years after Bakken defined his company's purpose and course, his mission statement remains largely unchanged, a testament to his vision for Medtronic.

The financing and focus marked a turning point for Medtronic, which earned a profit of $73,000 in fiscal year 1962–1963, more than doubled it the next year, and grew rapidly after that. Medtronic had 65 percent of the worldwide pacemaker market by 1970. Yet financing and focus would have made no difference without the transformation of Earl Bakken from engineer to leader. Content to build devices, he had relied on Hermundslie for much of the front-office duties. When Hermundslie cut back on his involvement for health reasons, Medtronic's board of directors asked Bakken if he intended to continue creating products or become president of the company. Bakken chose management, relying on his board for advice and counsel and on his staff for handling the daily operations. He later admitted that if he hadn't stepped up, Medtronic would have folded.

Under Bakken's leadership, Medtronic's sales soared from $518,000 in 1962 to almost $10 million in fiscal year 1968. He threw himself into his new role, arriving for work early in the morning, leaving late at night, traveling regularly, even devoting weekends to company business. "I don't think there's any alternative when starting and building a business than to give it everything you have, regardless of the personal sacrifice and disruption to the family," Bakken wrote in his autobiography. "If you're not prepared for sacrifice and disruption, then you'd be well advised not to start a business." His leadership style emphasized guidance and encouragement: he encouraged his engineers to seek creative solutions guided by Medtronic's mission. He believed completely in his people and his products, and while such belief helped propel Medtronic to industry leadership, it also led to setbacks the company had to overcome.

The first setback was the loss of talented people who started their own companies and became competitors. Bakken's ability to help employees realize their potential led to several leaving Medtronic to launch medical-device companies, beginning with four employees who established Cardiac Pacemakers in 1972. The new company quickly grabbed 10 percent of the pacemaker market. At last count, former Medtronic employees had founded more than thirty-five separate companies.

In 1976 a Medtronic product called Xytron began to experience failures. Bakken firmly believed in the quality of his company's products and valued Medtronic's standing in the medical community. While Xytron units continued to short out, he had the company collect data to confirm the problem. By the time he ordered a recall, Medtronic's once invincible standing had evaporated. Within a few years the company's worldwide market share had dropped to 40 percent. Bakken and Medtronic responded to the loss by initiating a more disciplined approach to product development while continuing to introduce innovative products.

Earl Bakken stepped down as president in 1967, serving as chair of the board until he retired in 1989. One of the roles he always relished was meeting with new employees to describe how the company started and its mission and values. He gave each employee a bronze medallion with the Medtronic "Rising Man" symbol and the words "Toward Full Life" engraved on it, and asked the employees to commit to the company's mission with the words, "You are here not to make money for yourself or the company, but to restore people to full life."

This passion for using science to benefit people began when, as a young man, Bakken was urged by his minister to apply his interest in technology to serving humanity. From two very different sources of inspiration—Frankenstein and a pastor's urging—Earl Bakken created an enduring enterprise.

Jeno Paulucci

Jeno Paulucci once said that "only in America would it be possible for a man with a name like Jeno Francisco Paulucci, son of poor Italian immigrants, to get rich selling a Chinese food in a Scandinavian region. And then sell the food business to a tobacco company for $63 million, cash."

As with Bakken, character and career reflected early influences on Paulucci's life. In his case, the greatest influence was how hard his family worked to survive. Born in 1918, he lived in Aurora, Minnesota, until the age of six, when his family moved to Hibbing. His job as a young boy was to find coal for the family stove, so he made a small wagon out of spare parts, pulled it along nearby railroad tracks, and scavenged whatever lumps had fallen from coal cars. When mining officials told him to get off their premises, he ignored them. They learned that Paulucci's father worked in the mine and threatened to fire him if young Jeno didn't stop stealing coal. He agreed to stop, then waited until dusk when he could barely see the coal—and the watchmen couldn't see him.

One day, as the disconsolate boy returned home without coal, his wagon caught on a wood paving block. He kicked at the block, took a few steps, and then returned to pry it out. Soaked with oil, the block would make excellent fuel. He filled his wagon with blocks from streets that had been deserted as the city moved south and the mines took over the land. The young Paulucci's ability to adapt would become one of the qualities leading to his success as an entrepreneur.

Another quality, his innate understanding of what customers want, surfaced during an early sales experience. After graduating from high school at age sixteen in the midst of the depression, he took a job selling fruit and vegetables for a Duluth market. A broken refrigeration unit sprayed ammonia around the market's storeroom and onto eighteen crates of bananas. Bananas sold for nineteen cents for four pounds, but these bananas, though safe to eat, were now speckled brown from the chemical. The owner told Paulucci to sell the bananas for whatever he could get. He peeled one and tasted it, noticing a slightly exotic flavor from the ammonia. He got an idea: He piled the counter facing the street with bananas, placing a hand-lettered sign in front of them that read "Argentine Bananas." "Argentine bananas!" he shouted. "First time ever sold in Duluth! You've never tasted such delicious bananas in your life!" He asked a woman in the gathering crowd to taste one and to agree that she had never tasted anything like it before. Three hours later he had sold all eighteen crates for ten cents a pound.

Ingenuity, persuasion, and unrelenting determination set Paulucci apart from his peers. Intent on moving up, he went to work for a wholesale grocer in St. Paul, persuading the grocer to give him the largely untapped northern Minnesota sales territory. He accepted no salary but proposed a fifty-fifty split of the profit on what he sold. The grocer agreed. Paulucci drove from town to town and store to store, sleeping in his car and eating his samples. He showed local grocers how buying in bulk at

Jeno Paulucci. Photograph courtesy of Luigino's, Inc.

a discount and splitting the goods among several stores saved them money. He also helped them create promotions and set up displays to increase sales, building on his "Argentine bananas" insight to move products.

In one case he approached several of his customers about cans of large peas that a processor was trying to unload at eighty-five cents for a dozen cans. He found little interest, selling just fifty cases. Weeks later he pitched the same peas in a different way, noting that the grocers were buying cans containing peas of all sizes for $1.35 a dozen while he would sell them cans of peas all the same size for a dime less and set up special displays to promote them. The new approach generated six times the sales of his previous approach at forty cents more per dozen cans. "Offer a buyer a quality product and then convince him of the fact that he is getting his money's worth. It seldom fails. I have built my entire business on this premise," Paulucci said. He sold so much he negotiated a 60-40 split of the profits, eventually earning more than the company's president. When the company wanted to rectify that situation by putting him on a straight salary, Paulucci decided it was time to start his own business.

His new firm sold garlic, but unfortunately Paulucci found little demand for the product and his company failed, leaving him heavily in debt but hardly discouraged. He had heard that hotels and restaurants were buying bean sprouts to replace the fresh vegetables that were strictly rationed during the war. He had also learned that the sprouts could be grown indoors without soil. He decided to check it out. He punched a washtub full of holes to allow drainage and filled it with beans and water. A few days later he had such a foul-smelling mound of rotting beans he had to throw the entire mess out. He had not known that bean sprouts grow from mung beans and not soybeans.

A banker laughed at his request for a $2,500 start-up loan, so Paulucci secured the money from a local food broker. He and his partner, David Persha, found a facility, installed vats, bought beans, and hired Asian workers to tend them. Eastern food processors that bought the sprouts claimed spoilage, sending smaller payments for the cost of the "good" sprouts. Paulucci tested the processors' claims by monitoring baskets of bean sprouts for longer periods of time than delivery to the East would have taken and found no signs of spoiling.

Seeking a solution, Persha suggested they can the sprouts themselves, but cans were hard to find during the war. Paulucci liked the idea and got a pea canner to agree to can the sprouts if Jeno could get the cans. In Washington he appeared before the War Production Board as a representative of the Bean Sprout Growers' Association (an association comprised of Paulucci and Persha) and explained the industry's desperate need for containers. The board offered a half-million "obsolete" cans that had small imperfections. Paulucci was in business.

The pea canner canned the sprouts under the Foo Young name until May, when he had to can peas. Paulucci and Persha found an abandoned plant in Iron River, Wisconsin, bought it, and began canning their own sprouts. The War Production Board came up with another five million cans. With the loan repaid and the business profitable, Paulucci and Persha expanded into chop suey vegetables and chow mein. Paulucci thought the food was bland and asked his mother to spice it up. After experimenting with different spices she found a combination they liked—and consumers eagerly bought.

A series of setbacks in the late 1940s did not deter Paulucci. His canner sued him, claiming he was entitled to more money since Paulucci was charging distributors more for his product. Paulucci disagreed, refused to settle, and lost. The cannery burned down. He and Persha dissolved their partnership, with Paulucci eventually buying the business. Persha didn't believe Paulucci could survive on his own and almost every banker agreed with him, limiting Paulucci's financial options. Someone contacted the Internal Revenue Service about irregularities in Paulucci's books and he was audited, though no problems were found.

Through it all his business improved, he paid off the lawsuit and other debts, and he pursued rapid growth, expanding into such diverse areas as growing celery, fruits, and berries on the Iron Range; experimenting with carrots and cabbage; harvesting cattails for use as insulation; growing and processing wild rice; growing mushrooms indoors, then selling the used soil as "Living Earth"; launching a real estate company and a chain of restaurants; and adding products to his Chinese food line, including fried rice, frozen egg rolls, soy sauce, and fortune cookies.

And he continued to sell. Paulucci had decided it made sense to market chow mein and chop suey in three-pound containers rather than the traditional one-pound cans. He presented his idea to a large grocery chain but it had no interest, so he went to another with a different approach: the new can, lower cost, and special displays and advertising would give the grocery-chain buyer a reputation for being a merchandising innovator. Paulucci left with an order for 33,600 cans. He returned to the first grocery chain and told its buyer about his competitor's order. The buyer changed his mind. Paulucci left town with orders for 84,000 cans—a quarter-million pounds of chow mein and chop suey.

Like many entrepreneurs, Jeno Paulucci hated to delegate. When the ink on frozen-food containers started to run, the New York packaging firm sent an investigator who offered to refund the cost of the containers. Paulucci said that wasn't enough. Rather than sending someone to negotiate, he flew to New York, where the packaging firm's executives finally agreed to pay $25,000 in addition to the cost of the containers. Paulucci said it still wasn't enough. After hours of wrangling they brought in their lawyers. A few hours later, Paulucci left with a check for $300,000. A similar problem with TV dinner trays that produced an unpleasant odor when placed in the oven elicited the same response from the tray manufacturer, similar discussions, and a nearly identical result: Paulucci received a check for $325,000. "We didn't make any money in either of these cases," he commented. "We simply avoided crippling the company. At times like these, timidity can easily cost one his business."

When he decided to change the name of his products and his company, he didn't delegate the task. He didn't even give it a lot of thought. After handing a Duluth printer an order for chow mein labels, the printer asked him what name to use on the labels. Paulucci wanted a new name and the Chinese capital at that time came to mind, so he suggested Chungking. When the printer told him he would never get a copyright on it, Paulucci wrote the name on a pad, studied it, crossed out the first *g*, and split it into two words: Chun King.

A stickler for strict quality control, he solved the problem of mushy chow mein by putting the vegetables in one can and the meat in another. Paulucci and his advertising agency decided to package the two cans together and call it Divider-Pak. One meeting. No market research. A new procedure that was ready to go in two weeks at a cost of $500, producing Divider-Paks that ended up accounting for much of Chun King's growth in the 1950s.

Jeno Paulucci sold his company to R. J. Reynolds in 1966 for $63 million. He was named chair of the Reynolds Food board. When he showed up for work at the company's New York headquarters at 6:00 A.M. the guard would not let him in the building; Paulucci could not believe people started work at 9:00. Never happy in the big corporation, he resigned after three years.

Before using the cash from selling Chun King to start a new frozen-pizza company, Jeno's Inc., Paulucci gave $2 million to his Chun King employees to help them pursue their own dreams and to thank them, he later said, "for not bugging me about a goddamn bowling league."

In *Jeno F. Paulucci, Merchant Philanthropist*, Paulucci summarized the lessons he had learned while building an enduring enterprise: "You have to know how to discipline yourself, to communicate and control. At times you have to be devious—I don't

A Chun King product display. Photograph courtesy of Luigino's, Inc.

mean dishonest. I mean you have to know how to zig when your competitor expects you to zag. You have to have an unquenchable appetite for success—the entrepreneur is always reaching for new challenges."

Rose Totino

Despite the similarities between Rose Totino and Jeno Paulucci—born and raised in Minnesota, children of poor Italian immigrants, leaders of companies that at one time made the best-selling pizza in the country, recipients of millions of dollars from selling their companies to large corporations—their differences affirm that entrepreneurial success does not depend on one particular path or personality type. Paulucci was a hustler; Totino was a housewife. Paulucci maintained control; Totino delegated. Paulucci ventured into Chinese food about which he initially knew nothing; Totino made pizza she had grown up with as a child.

Today it is hard to imagine a time when pizza was not a Minnesota staple, but that time is not far past. In fact, it was a novelty when Jim and Rose Totino were married in 1934. Both had dropped out of school at age sixteen to support themselves and their families, Jim working in a bakery and Rose doing housework. They had children and became involved in the community, having friends over to their home after PTA meetings and other events. The Totinos frequently served pizza, and their friends liked the food so much they would ask Rose if she could make pizzas for their social gatherings. "They'd offer to pay," Rose Totino said, "but how could you take money from friends and family?"

After World War II ended, returning soldiers who had discovered pizza in such places as New York, California, and Italy wondered why they could not get it in Minnesota. The Totinos recognized an opportunity, figuring they would need $1,500 to start their own pizza place. They called a banker about a loan and the banker, after

Rose Totino prepares pizza in the early 1950s.

asking what pizza was, set up a meeting with the loan committee. Rose brought a portable oven to the bank, set it up in the lunchroom, baked a pizza, and served it to the committee. They granted the loan.

The Totinos opened their carryout business in February 1951, and on their first day the line of customers stretched nearly three blocks. By the end of the day the Totinos were so exhausted they just stuffed their earnings into a brown bag without counting it. The next day, after they paid their bread, meat, milk, and ingredient suppliers, Rose said, "Jim, look, there's money left over after we paid all the bills. We must be profitable!" The Totinos remained profitable and exhausted for ten years, saving $5,000 a year by working eighteen- to twenty-hour days.

Their carryout business quickly evolved into a restaurant. "The boys from the service station would come over and say, 'Give me a fork. I'll eat here standing up.' So we put in a card table for the boys and at noon there would be a mad scramble for the card table," Rose said. They added tables until they had nine filled with people using plastic forks to eat out of cartons. Realizing she was running a restaurant, Rose had the shelving removed and tables and chairs installed. When the roofing company next door went out of business the Totinos expanded into the space, doubling their restaurant's size.

In 1961, with $50,000 in the bank, the Totinos faced a decision. Jim wanted to relax, travel, and maybe get in a little hunting and fishing. Rose pointed out that he was only forty-five years old and that he would be looking for something to do within a year. Rather than retire, they considered a new business: frozen pizza. They had opened a pizza place because of the enthusiasm of their first customers: their friends. They had grown into a restaurant because of the needs of their customers. Now they explored the market for frozen pizza because customers complained about having to travel across town to their restaurant for the pizza they loved.

The Totinos learned two facts about the potential market: (1) the frozen-food sections in most supermarkets were very small; and (2) Chef Boyardee made the only available frozen pizzas. They knew they could make a better pizza, but Jim realized that to do so they would need a crust bakery that cost $150,000. Since they also needed to pay for a facility and other start-up costs, they decided to start with frozen pasta entrées. They bought a production plant for $140,000, using all of their savings as a down payment on the facility and to buy ingredients. They began production in January 1962.

They agreed to an $80,000 advertising campaign to promote their new frozen-food line, but the campaign didn't work. By the end of the summer they had lost $150,000 and were near bankruptcy. That fall Jim attended a frozen-food convention where he learned about prebaked crusts, a breakthrough that eliminated the need for a crust bakery. Rose hated the crusts but acknowledged that other companies were using them successfully. A bigger problem was the $50,000 they required to switch production to pizza and pay for packaging equipment.

Someone told them about the Small Business Administration and they applied

Totino's restaurant on West Lake Street in Minneapolis, 1957. Photograph by Norton and Peel. Courtesy of the Minnesota Historical Society.

for a $50,000 loan. While they waited, they started making pizzas using an old phonograph turntable Jim had modified with a nozzle to add tomato sauce as the crust turned. "You'd push the foot pedal and the pizza would turn around once on the record player and be covered with sauce," Rose remembered. "Then you'd put another one on. The only trouble was, you got a shock every time you touched the pedal."

They made seventy-five cases of pizza the first day. They replaced the turntable with a commercial model built by a nearby engineering company for $500, but without the SBA loan they knew they were out of business. Even after the loan was granted they had to manage areas of the business such as distribution, sales, and marketing that they knew nothing about. Rose learned by asking questions and adding talent. "I surrounded myself with good people, and I hoped I could motivate them to do a good job for me—to make them feel needed and loved and part of the team," Rose said.

Their business took off. Rose called on buyers, pizza oven in hand to prepare samples, and quickly added distributors in the Twin Cities, Milwaukee, and Denver. At the same time, she and her employees continued to put toppings on their pizzas by hand. "In the third or fourth month of operations we made $100,000," Rose said. "I went out to the plant and announced, 'Let's put a little extra meat on each pizza.

We don't have to make all that money.'" As demand grew they added a second shift. Someone offered them $1 million for their business but they declined. Totino's Frozen Pizza became the top-selling pizza in the United States.

In 1970, with Rose as chief executive officer, the company opened a new, larger facility. "We were just growing out of the profits, but we were so heavily leveraged that we had to make money with the first order in the market," Rose said. Her management team discussed building multimillion-dollar plants on the East and West Coasts to grow the company, but the financial burden such expansion would create, together with Jim's failing health, led her to accept Pillsbury's offer of $22 million in common stock for Totino's. She became a vice president at Pillsbury. At the age of sixty, Rose Totino, the daughter of poor Italian immigrants who had entered the workforce doing housework for $2.50 a week, became a multimillionaire and one of the top female executives in the world.

The years following World War II were a golden age for Rose Totino and other entrepreneurs in Minnesota. Manny Fingerhut pioneered direct marketing to consumers forty years before Michael Dell popularized the approach with computers, founding Fingerhut Companies in 1948. In 1949 Fred Remmele used his life savings to start Remmele Engineering, a tool-and-die company built upon the skills and ideas men had gained from their military training. In Warroad, Bill Marvin considered the livelihoods of his four younger brothers returning from the war, as well as those of other area soldiers, and decided that the lumberyard his father had founded should concentrate on windows. In Roseau in 1956, Edgar and Allan Hetteen pioneered the snowmobile industry with the first Polaris snowmobile. Edgar later moved to Thief River Falls to build Arctic Cat snowmobiles.

Curt Carlson's Gold Bond Stamps took off in 1953 when Supervalu placed its first order. Following the sudden death of her husband in 1955, Ebba Hoffman took over an office-products manufacturer struggling with $4 million in revenues and led Smead Manufacturing through consolidation, acquisition, and customer service to $300 million in revenues in 1998. Oscar Howard, son of a Georgia sharecropper, started Howard Industrial Catering in Minneapolis in 1956, designed and patented food-warming devices, helped originate the Meals on Wheels program to feed the elderly, and was the first African American president of the Minnesota Restaurant Association. Alan "Buddy" Ruvelson, who founded First Midwest Capital Corporation in 1959, led the venture-capital revolution by handling the first leveraged buyout and making the first investment in a software firm.

Marvin Schwan

Though too young to serve in the war, Marvin Schwan grew up quickly in the postwar boom. He left college in 1950 to run his father's ice-cream store in Marshall, Minnesota. Two years later, forced by a price freeze on milk to sell it for less than he was buying it, the business nearly closed. Schwan wanted to marry a Montevideo woman, but he needed to offer something more than a failing business. Insight and experience presented an opportunity.

First, he noticed that ice cream cost more in Montevideo and other towns than in

Marvin Schwan. Photograph courtesy of Schwan's.

One of Schwan's first creamy yellow delivery trucks. Photograph courtesy of Schwan's.

Marshall. If he could sell his father's ice cream in these communities, he could make a profit. Second, he knew a lot of farmers were buying home freezers they could use to stock up on frozen goods. Third, he understood a little about home delivery from a milk route he had when he was fourteen. Schwan bought a panel truck for $100, filled it with dry ice and fourteen gallons of his father's ice cream, and sold every gallon his first day. The potential of this new business was all the encouragement he needed to get married later that year.

When he couldn't keep up with demand, he bought another truck and had it painted creamy yellow, a color that remains synonymous with Schwan's trucks in Minnesota. Today, home delivery of Schwan's foods is available in all forty-eight states in the continental United States.

In 1970 Marvin Schwan bought Kansas-based Tony's Pizza. He improved the recipe and marketed the pizza directly to retail stores through a special fleet of trucks. By the 1980s, nearly half of Schwan's sales came from pizza. Totino's, which had been bought by Pillsbury, had 22 percent of the national market share, while Tony's and Jeno's (Jeno Paulucci's pizza) each had 13 percent. Marvin Schwan continued to aggressively build his company until his death in 1993.

Growing the Business (1965–2000)

Joel Ronning

In the aftermath of the Vietnam War and civil rights protests of the 1960s, the American economy tanked. The confidence of the 1950s and early 1960s gave way to a collective angst fueled by losing a war, confronting racial prejudice, and nearly impeaching a president. An oil embargo aggravated the situation by forcing drivers to conserve the gasoline they had to wait in line to buy. Interest rates and unemployment soared. The stock market stagnated.

Joel Ronning started his first company in the worst of times, selling auto parts to dealers while attending the University of Minnesota in the mid-1970s. Within a year he was earning more in his spare time than his father made as a full-time high-school teacher, and he left college to build his business. He found he could buy Mercedes-Benz automobiles for $10,000 less in Canada than in the United States and began importing and selling them. "I was buying truckloads and selling them in Texas, Florida, and California," Ronning recalled, "making piles of money and driving a brand-new Mercedes."

As with so many entrepreneurs profiled in this book, his fortunes changed with the economy. High interest and unemployment rates, dubbed "stagflation," ultimately caused a recession in the early 1980s. "What had been easy became a real challenge," Ronning said. "I realized that the market for the Mercedes had just vaporized." In true entrepreneurial fashion he looked at what he was doing from a fresh perspective. While buying and selling Mercedes-Benzes, he had discovered that the manufacturer had no way of informing dealers about what cars were available in the system. Ronning had been using a little Apple computer to manage his business and saw a way to take

Joel Ronning. Photograph courtesy of Digital River, Inc.

advantage of the technology. He had two people call every Mercedes dealership in the United States to get a list of every car in stock, compiled the list on his computer, and sent it to nearly fifteen hundred dealerships in the United States and Canada. Tell us what you want, he advised, and we'll get it to you.

His insight paid the bills and awakened him to the power of technology. "These guys were using Stone Age tools," Ronning said. "They didn't even have fax machines back then. I figured out that I just did what Mercedes couldn't do and what tremendous capabilities it had. I became enthralled with the technology."

He drew upon his importing experience to bring in Apple IIe peripherals from Taiwan and Canada and sell them in the United States. He developed one of the first Apple-compatible portable computers shortly before Apple introduced its own, which doomed Ronning's product. When the Macintosh came out in 1984 he developed disk drives and other storage products for it.

In 1985 he founded Mirror Technologies to market Macintosh peripherals. The business went from zero to $12 million in revenues in its first year, but it grew too fast. "I knew marketing but didn't understand operations," Ronning remembered. "We had a bunch of investors come in and take over the operation. I got bored." He left Mirror

Technologies to become a partner in a California software company, where he learned about software development and architecture.

In 1990 he started Tech Squared, a catalog-distribution company of computer software and peripherals. "The first guy I hired was an accountant," said Ronning, alluding to the lessons he had learned at Mirror. "I spent all of my time in the back room in manufacturing, learning [management guru W. Edwards] Deming's processes for quality, focusing on the quality and the repeatability of processes." The focus paid off. Tech Squared soared from $40,000 in revenues its first year to $46 million in 1994. Ronning bought his old company, Mirror Technologies, for a nickel on the dollar and ran what had been a one-hundred-person operation with just fifteen people. "It turned out to be a tremendous acquisition that allowed us to grow quickly and to be massively profitable," he said.

Tech Squared grew as a sluggish American economy recovered from another recession, this one stimulated by the 1991 Gulf War. As the economy accelerated and the stock market took notice, Ronning moved in a new direction. He knew software and computers were evolving too fast for his catalog business to keep up. Applying what he had learned during his brief stint with the California software company, he developed a method of encrypting software to protect it from illegal distribution and putting it on hard drives for customers to try. Fujitsu, one of Tech Squared's largest suppliers, recognized the potential of the encryption technology. With Fujitsu's financial support and Ronning's technology, Ronning started Digital River in 1994, selling Tech Squared to his new company. "An entrepreneur has some level of vision that others don't," Ronning said. "This plus that equals opportunity. When you've got your eye on it, when you can connect the dots, you don't care. When I knew how it all needed to come together, it was crystal clear. I was shocked that others couldn't see it."

Flash back to Joel Ronning's first experience connecting the dots. A young college student eager to broaden his experiences, he joined the University of Minnesota's sailing club, a tiny group of fourteen people with four boats. "The U at that time was fifty thousand students, and I thought, 'My gosh, what a shame [that more of them don't know about the club],'" he said. Ronning figured that many more students interested in sailing might join if only they knew the club existed. The club's leader recognized Ronning's interest and asked him to head the group. Over the next two years Ronning built the sailing club into the second-largest club on campus, organizing sailing training for the ROTC, conducting membership and fund-raising drives, expanding the club's fleet to thirty-eight boats, starting an intercollegiate racing team, and increasing the club's budget from $10,000 to $250,000. "We always brought in more than we spent," he said. "My motivation wasn't personal—just the excitement and fulfillment of it. I was only twenty years old. It was very exciting."

Although he excelled at organizing and promoting and connecting the dots—"The need with the ROTC just seemed patently obvious to me," he remembered—Ronning also learned. "I think one of the things I figured out was to listen a lot," he said, "to be aware that a lot of people have good ideas." Twenty years later that experience would help him create an e-commerce leader.

In 1995 Joel Ronning saw the potential of delivering software over the Internet, which at that time consisted of a few networks such as AOL (America Online), Prodigy, and CompuServe. "In 1996 it started to get some traction," he said. "We really started building the organization then. In 1996 we were counting clients in the tens, in 1997 by the hundreds, and today we have eight thousand."

Digital River manages e-commerce for some of the largest software companies in the world, providing services that include fulfillment, merchandising, marketing, and building customer relationships. Of the top one hundred software companies, forty-six outsource their e-commerce business. Digital River handles thirty-nine of them while the remaining seven are split among four competitors.

Digital River went public on August 11, 1998. Although it had already spent $4 million to $5 million building its infrastructure, it now had $75 million and a mandate to grow. "We spent at an ungodly rate on equipment, facilities, and people," Ronning said. "It was really scary. In the back of my mind I asked how we could spend this kind of money. It was an enormous responsibility because tens of thousands of people were involved in that money."

From 1996 to 2000, investors went nuts over Internet companies. The electronic land rush to claim virgin e-territory sought rapid growth above all else, including profits. Spend more. Spend faster. And keep spending. "The rules changed during that period," Ronning said. "I couldn't believe how big the bubble was. I don't think I'll ever see that kind of opportunity again. There was huge pressure to act even if it's wrong. Had it happened ten years earlier, none of us, not me or my team, would have been prepared."

Digital River grew its software division at breakneck pace for four years until the dot-com bubble burst. The company added approximately 280 new clients a month until the middle of 1999. Although it continues to acquire new clients, its focus for the past two years has been on refining the organization to make it more efficient.

In 1999 the company launched an e-commerce division, targeting large companies not in the software business. "Our goal is to be *the* global e-commerce outsourcing leader," Ronning said. "We're on that path. We've been getting triple-digit growth from inception, and our goal is to double sales next year. Our job now is to convince large companies that they need to be selling through the Internet and to outsource through us."

Digital River's client list currently includes 3M, *National Geographic,* Coors, Fox Interactive, Hasbro, Staples.com, Major League Baseball, Siemens, and Nabisco. It develops and markets its clients' sites; creates the security, ordering, and fulfillment systems; and handles such matters as customer service and product returns. Providing these services requires a tremendous investment in infrastructure, something the late-1990s bubble made possible. Nabisco, for example, chose Digital River because of its infrastructure, specifically its data center, hosting capability, order-management capability, and experience developing nearly seventy-five hundred e-commerce storefronts for other large companies. "When clients select a company they look at its balance sheet, stability, and references," Ronning said. "They want to be in the club with the other Fortune 50 guys. Satisfied clients reap a larger group of satisfied clients."

While many Internet companies spent millions on infrastructure during the 1990s, only a few have survived a plummeting stock market and vanishing venture capital. Digital River continues to grow, and Ronning knows why: "We had an advantage from the start because this isn't the first one of these things I've done. This group was handpicked for their experience in industry. And we're prudent. At the companies we've bought, we go in and everybody's sitting in $1,000 chairs and they've got a hundred employees and they're wondering why they're out of cash. When we started we bought used stuff or borrowed equipment from Tech Squared. We crunched more people into smaller space. We're just not going to go crazy; that's part of our culture. Our competitors haven't achieved that level of focus and aren't as careful about their spending habits."

Ronning delivered a business plan in 1998 that called for Digital River to be profitable in the fourth quarter of 2001. Although the Internet frenzy fizzled shortly after the plan was written, Digital River achieved the goal. Two other achievements attest to the unusually robust company he has built: Digital River has a client retention rate of 97 percent and has never had to lay off workers.

To retain employees, the company has a director of corporate culture and training to manage such perks as Beer Friday—free beer from 4:00 to 6:00 P.M. every Friday—

On one day each month, Digital River employees can bring their dogs to work. Photograph courtesy of Digital River, Inc.

and Dog Day, the one Thursday each month when employees can bring their dogs to work. Ronning equates running the company to being mayor of a community of four hundred. His focus has shifted to management, team development, organizational-structure development, and strategy. "I spent a lot of time putting my executive team of fifteen vice presidents together because everything then takes care of itself," he says. "I'm much more dependent on my managers than when I started the company."

"Business fundamentals don't change in the Internet world," Ronning advises. "Forget the end of the 1990s. That world won't come back. Now you've got to be profitable right away or you probably can't get funded. When I started this company in 1994, the landscape was a lot like it is today. It was funded by a partner that had strategic interests. Raw technology that changes the fundamentals of how things are done will continue to be funded, but concepts aren't being funded anymore."

It's easy for today's budding entrepreneurs to believe that the best opportunities still exist in an Internet-related business. In the late 1990s little else appeared on the radar screens of businesspeople and investors alike. When the bubble burst, day traders returned to their day jobs while Internet entrepreneurs looked for new jobs. The sudden turnaround dashed the dreams of many who felt a rich future was only one bright idea and a few years away.

As the entrepreneurs profiled in this book have shown, many paths lead to unimagined success, and when one path disappoints, others offer promising possibilities. Consider Circuit City, the best-performing stock of the 1980s. If you had invested $10,000 in its stock in 1980 and held onto it, your stock would have been worth nearly $1 million in 1990. Amazingly, the stock of Circuit City's chief competitor delivered an even better return in the 1990s. While new investors and entrepreneurs flocked to such well-publicized tech stories as Cisco Systems, Microsoft, Dell, and AOL, two retail chains earned astounding returns on investment.

Circuit City held the edge it had built during the 1980s until 1997, when it slipped to second place in its industry behind a company that had not been incorporated until 1985. The revenues of that company, Best Buy, had rocketed from $9 million in 1982 to $7 billion in 1996, propelled by an entrepreneur whose vanity license plates read DRIVEN: Richard Schulze.

Richard Schulze

In the summer of 1981 a tornado peeled off the roof of the Sound of Music electronics store in Roseville. The store was the largest in a chain of eleven started by Dick Schulze in 1966. The tornado scattered televisions and stereos to nearby parking lots and fields while exposing to the elements the products that remained. Schulze, already feeling the competitive pressure from larger discount chains, had no business-interruption insurance. A liquidator bought the store's inventory, but in one of those rare, "connect-the-dots" moments, Schulze bought it all back and spent his entire $25,000 marketing budget on thousands of flyers and radio spots to promote a "Tornado Sale." He erected a huge tent on the store's parking lot. On the day of the sale he closed his other stores to allow all sixty-five Sound of Music employees to sell the drastically reduced merchandise.

The sale drew so many shoppers Schulze had to fetch TVs and stereos from his other stores to meet the demand. The event "tied up traffic on [Interstate] 94 for miles," Schulze says. "It was awesome." It was also illuminating. "It was an opportunity to really understand why a new strategy would in fact be more exciting and more meaningful for us," Schulze says. "It made it easier to make the move from Sound of Music to Best Buy because we had this real-life example of how consumers will react to real opportunity."

Two years after the tornado, Schulze renamed his company Best Buy to appeal to an older, broader, and more affluent customer base. He opened his first superstore in Burnsville, financing it by using his home and business as collateral. It was no small risk: located in what, at the time, still seemed a fairly remote area, the new store had to do more business than the whole chain had been doing just to break even. It wasn't the first huge risk Schulze had taken, nor would it be his last. "'Succeed or die' is a powerful motivator," he says.

Dick Schulze started Sound of Music, a small stereo shop in St. Paul, in 1966 with $9,000 from a second mortgage on his house. A graduate of St. Paul's Central High School, he had received extensive electronics training while serving the U.S. Air Force

Richard Schulze. Photograph courtesy of Best Buy Company, Inc.

as a member of the Minnesota Air National Guard. Following his discharge he sold consumer-electronics components in a four-state area as an independent manufacturer's representative. After six years of selling, he and a partner opened Sound of Music.

In the first year they expanded to three stores. Schulze bought out his partner in 1970 and continued to add more stores throughout the decade. In 1980 intense competition from discount chains put Sound of Music within days of bankruptcy. Schulze responded by convincing creditors to wait a few weeks for payment and borrowing enough cash from his family to keep the doors open. He decided he had to expand his product lines to offer appliances and VCRs, a costly gamble he funded by persuading suppliers to waive the rights to their own inventory, which he then used as collateral to secure a $100,000 credit line. His business survived.

By offering a greater variety of products at discount prices through the new Burnsville superstore and seven other stores in the Upper Midwest, Best Buy claimed 42 percent of the local market. The Burnsville store alone had sales exceeding $1 million for its grand opening weekend, more than any of Schulze's smaller stores had sold in an entire year—tangible proof that the superstore concept worked. By 1987 Best Buy had twenty-four stores, sales of $239 million, and earnings of $7.7 million.

Sales nearly doubled the following year, but earnings dropped 64 percent because of price wars triggered by growing competition from such chains as Highland Superstores. Once again, Schulze imagined a new future for his enterprise, an approach he called Concept II.

Concept II responded to Schulze's view of what most shoppers wanted: less sales help and hassle-free buying, which meant no service-plan contracts, no waiting for merchandise to come from the back room, and no switching from counter to counter to get help. He implemented Concept II in his stores over the next few years, increasing floor space, stocking more items on the floor, reducing the number of salespeople, offering more self-help product information and an Answer Center for those who needed assistance, and providing one-stop purchasing. He also moved his sales force from commission to salary, a controversial decision that cost the chain contracts with major manufacturers such as Kenwood, Whirlpool, and Hitachi, who feared lower profit margins and a more competitive sales environment. Despite fewer product choices, consumers loved Concept II. Shoppers stayed in the stores an average of a half-hour per visit, nearly double their time in Best Buy's first stores.

In April 1991 Highland conceded defeat and closed its stores. A change in Best Buy's accounting method contributed to a loss of $9.4 million that fiscal year, but the end of the price wars and the deployment of Concept II spurred dramatic growth. Best Buy opened thirty-eight new stores in 1992. Revenues had climbed from $929 million in 1992 to $1.6 billion in 1993 when Circuit City, the eight-hundred-pound gorilla in consumer electronics, decided it was time to confront Best Buy on its home turf. At the time, Circuit City was larger and more stable than Best Buy, with a history of wider profit margins and little debt. In comparison, Best Buy's debt-to-capital ratio in 1993 stood at 43 percent. Another price war broke out.

Best Buy didn't flinch. Schulze created Concept III, even larger superstores that offered a greater selection of some products and interactive technology for the consumer's convenience. Although the new concept failed to generate the excitement of its predecessor, Best Buy's revenues jumped to $3 billion in fiscal 1995 and $7 billion the next year as it rose to within one-tenth of 1 percent of Circuit City's market share. But the pursuit of sales came at the expense of profits. Best Buy's earnings dropped from $58 million in 1995 to less than $2 million in 1997. Falling computer prices and a soft consumer-electronics market contributed to the shortfall.

The 1996 holiday season proved particularly difficult. Anticipating strong demand for personal computers, Schulze loaded up on $300 million in computers before learning that Intel planned to announce the introduction of a faster Pentium microprocessor. He met with Intel chair Andrew Grove to try to delay the announcement until after the holiday buying season, but Grove refused. The prospect of buying a soon-to-be-obsolete computer discouraged shoppers from making the purchase, and Best Buy was stuck with millions of dollars worth of outdated computers.

Two days after Christmas Dick Schulze's father died, only eight months after the death of his mother. The deaths, the holiday computer fiasco, and the mediocre performance of the Concept III stores hit Schulze hard, and he took two weeks off to think about the future of his company. When he returned he developed a two-year plan to deliver more help to customers, better training for employees, and greater value for shareholders. He then hired an outside consulting firm to help the company reinvent itself. After careful study, the firm recommended a slowdown in expansion plans, a reduction in product mix, and the replacement of dozens of senior executives, many chosen and mentored by Schulze. "Entrepreneurs have to come to grips with [the fact] that sometimes there will be no one in your organization who has the right skill sets or experiences that relate to your plan, no matter how good you think your people are or how much you've accomplished in the past," Schulze said. He followed the recommendations, and Best Buy recovered to post earnings of $82 million in 1998.

Expansion plans were brought back on line and broadened. The company determined that expansion to 650 stores by 2004 would approach the maximum coverage that made sense in the United States. To continue to grow it would have to penetrate international markets and acquire other companies.

In 2001 Best Buy opened eight stores in Canada, with plans to add another thirty stores by 2004. To accelerate its position it bought Future Shop and its eighty-eight stores in Canada. It acquired Musicland and its thirteen hundred stores to gain access to young consumers through such stores as Sam Goody and Suncoast, and bought Magnolia Hi-Fi to establish an immediate presence in the Seattle area. Speaking to stock analysts in a December 2000 conference call, Schulze emphasized how these plans served the company's vision "to be at the many intersections where consumers find their lives connecting with technology. . . . We're going to go where we have to go to be the best in the business."

Which Best Buy currently is, having passed Circuit City as the industry leader in 1997. It has also been a leader in giving back to the community. "I've made no secret of the fact that I think entrepreneurs, for the most part, accumulate the greatest wealth in this country," Schulze says. "And those, I believe, are more inclined to give back to where they came from."

In 2000 Dick Schulze and his wife, Sandra, gave the University of St. Thomas $50 million, the largest gift in the St. Paul school's history and the largest donation ever reported to a Minnesota college or university. Schulze had grown up in the St. Thomas neighborhood and two of his four children had attended the university. That same year Schulze gave 1.5 percent of Best Buy's profits of $347 million to charity. An active leader in United Way, he has received several awards for service, including America's Promise Red Wagon for Community Service awarded by Colin Powell in 1999 and the 1999 Corporate Leader of the Year by the Juvenile Diabetes Foundation.

When presenting the gift to St. Thomas, Schulze said, "We realize that this institution shares our entrepreneurial approach to life. . . . The people at St. Thomas realize that accomplishment is the product of calculated and managed risk. It is a result of the strong desire to deliver value and service to the community. Best Buy was also built on these ideals."

Like Joel Ronning, William Norris, Earl Bakken, Sister Antonia McHugh, and many other Minnesota entrepreneurs, Dick Schulze built an enduring enterprise by taking risks. While the risks may have been calculated and managed, these entrepreneurs still bet everything on their visions of the future. "Succeed or die," Schulze said. Most die; since Best Buy was formed, nearly six hundred competitors have gone out of business.

While the sudden demise of so many promising Internet companies has dominated recent headlines, no company is guaranteed a smooth path or a long life. The entrepreneurs who create enduring enterprises exhibit an almost irrational confidence in both their dreams and their abilities, adapting quickly and wisely when circumstances change, discovering, as Goethe wrote, that "boldness has genius, power, and magic in it." Too often, confidence and boldness are the only arrows in the entrepreneur's quiver.

Leeann Chin

At the age of forty-seven, Leeann Chin opened her own restaurant, serving Cantonese and Szechuan food. Her in-laws advised against it and her husband predicted she would fail because she lacked the training to run a restaurant. But she also had supporters.

After sampling her cuisine at catering events, actor Sean Connery invested in her business, as did banker Carl Pohlad. The Small Business Administration loaned her money. Bonaventure Mall in Plymouth welcomed her, although it had initially asked her to open a cooking school in the building.

Chin decorated her restaurant with Oriental artifacts from her own collection. On opening day in 1980, with a crowd lined up for lunch, she discovered she had no lights and no working ovens. "The restaurant was full, so I took out my wok and started stir-frying the food for a buffet," she said. "I was worried, but the customers thought it was wonderful."

Adapt quickly. Succeed or die.

On the second day things got worse: a power failure shut down the shopping center during the dinner hour, dashing Chin's plans to serve a sit-down menu for dinner. Out came the wok again and with it a change in plans. "The customers asked me to keep it that way, and I have. Plus, the buffets make good business sense. I can buy for a day-to-day menu that revolves around the freshest available vegetables," she said. Like the tornado that exposed Dick Schulze to a new and better way of doing business, Chin's power problems helped her discover what her customers wanted. She adapted quickly and her restaurant thrived, grossing more than $1.5 million in its first year.

A critical factor in any entrepreneur's ability to adapt is experience. Joel Ronning has successfully steered Digital River through the turbulent Internet seas by drawing on nearly two decades of experience in the industry. Leeann Chin had been cooking since she was a child, managed a sewing and alterations business from her home, taught Chinese cooking since 1972, and catered parties and receptions.

Born in Canton, China, in 1933, Chin worked in her father's market counting sales on an abacus, delivering rice on her bicycle, ordering spices and herbs, and trying out recipes with the family's chef as her guide. She married Tony Chin when she was eighteen and moved to Minneapolis in 1956. Tony Chin worked at his sister's Minneapolis

Leeann Chin demonstrates stir-frying in a skillet and a wok, 1979. Copyright 2002 Star Tribune/ Minneapolis–St. Paul. Used by permission.

restaurant and Leeann Chin altered clothes for downtown department stores, even though she spoke no English. When she realized that their income would not be enough to get their five children through college, she began learning English while providing sewing and alterations from her home.

On occasion she served dinner to her clients. They asked her for her recipes and encouraged her to teach Chinese cooking, which she began doing at a friend's home. The classes were so popular she moved them to local schools, and her food was such a hit she quit her seamstress work to be a caterer.

Word of her culinary wizardry spread to the General Mills Creating Learning Center, which offered Chin a teaching position that she accepted and held until 1979. Minneapolis and St. Paul newspapers published her recipes. She appeared on local television shows. Catering exposed her to influential people such as Connery and Pohlad. In 1980 General Mills approached her about putting her recipes in a cookbook. Published in 1981, *Betty Crocker's Chinese Cookbook: Recipes by Leeann Chin* sold more than 350,000 copies worldwide.

All of these experiences helped Chin successfully launch her first restaurant, but her initial electrical problems soon seemed minor compared with the conflicts she had with investors over management and direction of the restaurant. A frustrated Chin offered to sell her share of the business. The investors declined, choosing instead to sell their interest to her. By late 1983 she had full control of her operation. She spent

Carl Pohlad invested in Leeann Chin's new restaurant, and Robert Redford enjoyed the cuisine. Photograph used with permission.

$300,000 adding 130 seats to the restaurant, then opened a second restaurant in downtown St. Paul. The new restaurant also exceeded $1.5 million in sales in its first year, while the Bonaventure restaurant's annual sales now topped $2 million. In 1984 Dayton's asked Chin to open a take-out service in its downtown Minneapolis department store. The operation soon averaged a thousand customers a day.

Expansion had not been part of her plans, but Chin chose to expand "for the sake of my crew members. I was concerned about their welfare, their future. They were satisfied but needed opportunities, so I realized I had to either expand or lose them. In the interest of my employees, as well as consumer demand, I began to consider the idea of expanding beyond my first restaurant."

By late 1984 Chin knew that further expansion demanded more financial resources and business expertise than she had. General Mills, which had approached her about a new cookbook, was gobbling up restaurant chains, including Red Lobster and Olive Garden. It offered to buy her business and turn it into a national chain. Excited by the prospect, she sold her operation to General Mills and joined the company as president of Leeann Chin, Inc.

A third restaurant opened in Minneapolis followed by others in the Twin Cities and in Illinois. Chin learned how large companies handled expansion. She also learned how large companies often deal with adversity. When the company's efforts to crack the Chicago market failed, it closed the Illinois restaurants and turned its attention to its other chains. Chin had no say in the decision. In 1988 General Mills decided that the business did not fit into its plans and sold it back to Chin. She has since said that selling her company was her greatest business mistake because it left her with little to do and no professional and personal challenges.

Back at the helm of the business she had started, Chin took charge quickly and decisively. She worked out an agreement with Byerly's, a large upscale supermarket chain, to sell her take-out food in its Twin Cities stores. Over the next six years she opened carryout locations in the Twin Cities and Seattle and a catering center while managing her three restaurants. She hired a former General Mills executive to be the president of her growing enterprise. By 1994 her company had more than seven hundred employees and annual revenue of $25 million.

Once again her plans to expand surpassed her financial resources. Three institutional investors provided $11 million to grow the business in exchange for slightly more than 50 percent of the company. The company's president used some of the capital to open Asia Grille restaurants, which featured food from five Asian countries, a take-out counter, and a small Oriental market. The new concept failed. Worse yet for Chin, the investors worked closely with the president while ignoring Chin. In January 1996 she took a leave of absence from the company only to return a year later, one month after the president resigned, to head the board of directors.

The board dropped the Asia Grille concept in early 1998. A new chief executive officer, Stephen Finn, acknowledged that the concept was a "huge strategic blunder" that almost "bankrupted the company." He also recognized Chin's value to the company. "She is the brand, the master chef, the external relations, the teacher," Finn said.

"She is a major asset who will help raise awareness of the brand and guard against being just a new Chinese restaurant in new markets."

In an age when branding has become paramount, Chin boasts a loyal following. Every year since 1985, Leeann Chin has been voted "Best Chinese Food" and "Best Takeout Food" in Minneapolis. By 2001 her chain of forty-five locations employed fifteen hundred people and had annual sales of $50 million.

Like Dick Schulze and Best Buy, Chin and her company survived the peaks and valleys of starting and growing a business while finding time to give back to the community. In 2000 alone, she served on the boards of the College of St. Benedict, Boy Scouts of America, Lowertown Redevelopment Corporation, and the Minnesota Vikings Advisory Board. She is a member of the Committee of 100, a national organization giving voice to Chinese Americans. She created the Leeann Chin Foundation in 1995. In the communities where she has restaurants, she participates in organizations such as community-development committees, diversity advocacy groups, and the arts.

Leeann Chin follows a Minnesota tradition of creating an enduring enterprise around our need to eat, a tradition that started with Washburn and Pillsbury, who milled the wheat bought from Cargill and Peavey, that continued with the processors Hamm and Brandt, and that evolved into the food products provided by Totino, Paulucci, and Schwan. Joel Ronning built upon Minnesota's history of technological innovation first evident in the milling operations of Washburn and Pillsbury, embedded by McKnight in 3M's culture, and elevated to international prominence by Norris, Bakken, and many others.

Of course, not every exceptional entrepreneur fits neatly into a century-old Minnesota groove. Take Jimmy Jam Harris and Terry Lewis, for instance, who took the road less traveled in both their business and their partnership.

Jimmy Jam Harris and Terry Lewis

Jimmy Jam Harris and Terry Lewis have been friends since they were thirteen and business partners since they were twenty-three. They met in 1972 as part of a group of gifted junior-high students spending a summer in an Upward Bound program at the University of Minnesota. They discovered a mutual interest in music and formed an impromptu band that entertained the other students at an end-of-summer party, and they've been making music ever since.

Lewis played bass, Harris keyboard. In high school Lewis excelled as a state-champion track star and an all-city football player, but an injury his senior year convinced him that music offered less hazardous opportunities. He started a band called Flyte Tyme, named after a Donald Byrd lyric, playing clubs and dances and becoming an institution in Minneapolis. "Minneapolis is a very artsy city," Lewis said. "It offered us as a small, black 'performing' group the opportunity to expose ourselves to a limited clientele. We had to work very hard to get a gig. You had to be very proficient, and we didn't develop a lot of bad habits."

Terry Lewis (left) and Jimmy Jam Harris with Janet Jackson. Photograph courtesy of Flyte Tyme Productions.

At the age of fourteen Harris got the owner of a local roller rink to let him play the organ whenever the disc jockey took a break, then began spinning records himself. He parlayed that experience into a deejay spot at a Twin Cities radio station, where he developed his own style of playing along with the tunes on a keyboard. His popularity led to emcee jobs for R and B shows visiting town and deejay stints at a St. Paul teen club and Minneapolis adult dance clubs. He played with Lewis's Flyte Tyme band before starting his own band, Mind and Matter, for which he wrote music.

Flyte Tyme and Mind and Matter rivaled two other prominent Twin Cities bands of that day, Prince's Grand Central and drummer Morris Day's Enterprise Band of Pleasure. In 1981 the four men decided to combine their talents, forming The Time. The band's first single climbed to number six on the R and B charts. They went on a national tour from November of that year to April 1982.

Working together in the band helped Harris and Lewis learn about and appreciate each other's styles. They wrote music that didn't fit The Time's image, and that inspired them to seek new opportunities. "As much as I loved The Time, I always wanted more," Lewis said. "We were some broke, famous-being folks and I wanted to realize our potential. I said, 'We need to go to L.A. and make something happen.' And they told me I was crazy."

All except Harris. The two stayed with friends in Los Angeles while they recorded a simple demo of ten songs and networked with producers and musicians. Groups such as S.O.S. Band and Klymaxx picked up most of the songs, although Harris and

Lewis decided to hold onto the rights to their songs rather than sell them or sign them over to one label. Tabu president Clarence Avant liked what he heard and had them produce two tracks for S.O.S. Band over a weekend in Atlanta.

They continued to play in The Time, flying to L.A. and Atlanta during weekends to do their production work. Prince felt their outside work detracted from the band, but Harris and Lewis believed it would increase The Time's value. On their second tour the band finished playing in New York and faced four days off before its next stop in San Antonio. Harris and Lewis bolted to Atlanta to get in some production work for S.O.S. Band. An unexpected snowfall closed the airport, stranding the frantic duo in Atlanta. They missed the San Antonio performance, but no explanation was requested or given and the tour continued.

The fragile peace ended when photos of Harris, Lewis, and S.O.S. Band appeared in *Billboard* magazine. Prince called a meeting of band members to tell Harris and Lewis they were fired. The dejected partners drove to a nearby studio where they were scheduled to mix a song. When they told the engineer what had happened, he said, "I wouldn't worry about it—you've got a smash on your hands."

Before they could settle into their new full-time business, however, they had one more issue to resolve. "Terry was asked to come back [to The Time] and I wasn't," Harris said. "This was just before they were going to do *Purple Rain*. I told Terry, 'You should go back. It sounds kinda cool.' He said, 'Forget that! We're in this together.'"

They've been together ever since. One of the songs they were producing when they split with The Time held onto the number-two spot on the R and B charts for three weeks in 1983 and another climbed to number five. Their services suddenly in demand, the Flyte Tyme partners lived in a three-bedroom apartment in L.A. with their representative, recording in a basement studio. They moved back to the Twin Cities in 1984. Two years later a Janet Jackson album, *Control,* firmly established the reputations of producers Jimmy Jam Harris and Terry Lewis. The multiplatinum album delivered five number-one R and B hits and five Top 5 pop hits and earned Harris and Lewis their first Grammy as Producers of the Year. They have since earned Soul Train Music Awards, American Music Awards, five R and B and two pop ASCAP Songwriter of the Year Awards, an NAACP Image Award, eight platinum albums, eighteen gold albums, and fifteen gold singles, and have their own star on the Hollywood Walk of Fame.

They built a new studio in Edina in 1989. The following year they collaborated with Jackson to produce *Rhythm Nation: 1814,* an album that spawned the same number of hits as *Control.* In 1996 they formed a joint venture with Universal Records, with Harris and Lewis serving as cochairs of the new Flyte Tyme Records label.

Since 1982 Harris and Lewis have worked with dozens of contemporary artists in addition to Jackson, S.O.S. Band, and Klymaxx, including Human League, Nona Hendryx, Herb Alpert, Robert Palmer, Patti Austin, Gladys Knight, Patti LaBelle, Boyz II Men, Angel Grant, Kevin Ford, Mary J. Blige, Rod Stewart, Jon Secada, Michael Jackson, Lionel Ritchie, and Vanessa Williams. "We are fans of the artists we work with," Harris said. "We take the fact that we are fans and that we get the chance to shape what the next record will be. We try to do the kind of stuff we would like hearing [the artists] do because we want to be a fan of the records too."

Shaping an album takes no set path. In many cases Lewis writes the lyrics and Harris produces the track, but either may run with a project if he feels inspired. "If one of us does one project [on his own], the other listens to the mixes to make sure things fit, and at the end of the day it's always a Jam and Lewis production," Harris said. "We've worked this way since we started." They've also worked without a contract, splitting all profits equally. "That's what true partnership is," Lewis said. "We established that trust from the very beginning."

Such collaboration is uncommon among single-minded entrepreneurs who typically are unwilling or unable to share their vision. For Harris and Lewis, that vision includes a conscious decision not to become a much larger company, choosing to focus on making music rather than managing people.

Faced with the same decision, Glen Taylor chose the opposite path. "I am a hands-on type of person," he said, "and I was involved with everything. I knew that if this company was going to keep growing, it was going to have to go from an entrepreneurial sort of company to one where the managers had more leeway. . . . I thought that, given the opportunity, they would blossom, and I was right in that."

Annual revenues estimated at $1 billion verify the wisdom of Taylor's decision.

Glen Taylor

Glen Taylor became a state senator in 1980, in part to grow his business. Taylor Corporation was getting too big for one person to make all the decisions, yet his managers seemed hesitant to act on their own. By working in the Senate in St. Paul, Taylor separated himself from his company in Mankato, Minnesota. He still got daily reports. He still had a runner traveling between the two cities with important information. But he wasn't in Mankato, and his absence empowered people to decide and act. "I knew at the time that we had to go that way, that it had to work for us to grow the way we wanted to grow," Taylor said. "Did I believe we had the right people? Yes. Did I know it was going to work? No."

Running for Senate was, to use Dick Schulze's phrase, a calculated and managed risk. Although the outcome was not guaranteed, Taylor could draw upon twenty-five years of experience to anticipate its effect on his company, the first and only business he had worked for.

A farm boy from Comfrey, Minnesota, he enjoyed the athletic opportunities of a small town, playing football, basketball, track, and baseball until his senior year, when the responsibilities of a wife and baby daughter required him to earn money at neighboring farms. He enrolled in Mankato State in 1959 and found a part-time job at Carlson Craft, a small print shop that specialized in wedding invitations.

Taylor started at the bottom, stamping napkins. When another student took a leave of absence, Bill Carlson, the shop's owner, put Taylor in charge of the stockroom. He

Glen Taylor. In 1995, Taylor bought the NBA's Minnesota Timberwolves. Copyright 2002 Star Tribune/Minneapolis–St. Paul. Used by permission.

reengineered the inventory system to make it more efficient. His initiative caught Carlson's eye and Taylor's position at the company became permanent. Taylor's drive for efficiency extended to napkin stamping: He developed a stamping press with parts from a car, a stove's heating element, and a TV tube after first negotiating a cut of the profits from his invention.

He studied math, physics, and social studies in college and intended to be a teacher. He graduated from Mankato State in 1962, a year earlier than his peers, and interviewed for teaching jobs. Carlson encouraged him to explore the job market as long as Carlson had the chance to match any offer. During the interviews Taylor realized that he really wanted to be the boss, the principal or superintendent, a leadership position he already had as second-in-command at Carlson Craft. That desire to lead dawned at an early age, he recalls: "In first grade, I figured out teachers kept score, and from that time forward, I always wanted to know the highest score and if it was mine. I needed to be at the front of the line. Half the time I didn't even know what the line was for—but I wanted to be first to see where we were going." He told Bill Carlson he wanted to stay at his company at whatever salary Carlson offered. Carlson wrote "$4,200" on a piece of paper and Taylor thanked him, even though he had not had any teaching offers that low.

At that time, brides-to-be faced a choice in wedding invitations similar to the choice Henry Ford had offered Model T buyers: any color you want, as long as it's black. Black ink on ivory or white paper. Catholic or Protestant text. Printed when the printer has the time. Taylor listened to Mankato State students who told him they wanted options and faster service. He urged Carlson to offer different inks, papers, and text choices for wedding invitations and to shorten the delivery time. Carlson expanded the variety while Taylor reorganized the shop so that invitations were printed as soon as the orders arrived. "It seems so obvious now, but other people were printers while we were people getting the bride what she wanted," he said.

Although Carlson trusted Taylor's judgment, his conservative nature tempered the young man's ambition. "Everything I wanted to do he cut by a third, and then it was successful," Taylor said. "His experience and wisdom and my enthusiasm and risk-taking made for a successful business."

Taylor learned from his mentor and by experience. "I went out with a marketing program and sold way more than we could handle. We worked seven days a week, week after week, and I burned out the employees. And we didn't make any money. I learned you've got to balance everything. That helped me," he said. Taylor also learned by listening. "I quizzed everyone—suppliers, acquaintances, businesspeople I'd meet at a party," he said. "If you're sincere, if you're respectful, almost anyone will sit down and answer your questions. You don't have to make a lot of mistakes if you ask a lot of questions."

Carlson Craft grew dramatically in the 1960s, propelled by its customer-oriented culture, innovations in the printing industry, and broadening service in the Midwest from UPS. Bill Carlson started selling shares in the company to his three key employees, one of whom was Glen Taylor, in 1967. When Carlson retired in 1974 he sold his majority interest to Taylor with the blessing of his other two shareholders, who also sold Taylor a portion of their holdings.

In 1975 Taylor formed Taylor Corporation, a holding company in which Carlson Craft was the first subsidiary. He added other small printing companies with an elegant approach: he lowered the cost by paying cash and promising to retain the employees after the sale. If the promise was important to the seller, Taylor figured he would gain loyal employees. If the promise didn't matter, he walked away from the deal. The approach allowed Taylor to build his empire with almost no debt. "It comes down to why this company is here in the first place, and that's to provide security and opportunity for our employees," he said. "If I borrow, I'm letting a banker dictate how my business is run. And I'm not going to do that to myself or the people of this company."

In the late 1970s he handpicked a dozen managers to groom for leadership positions in his growing company. When he felt they were prepared to assume more responsibility, he ran for the Senate to "get out of their way." He was a state senator until 1986, the last two years serving as Senate minority leader. His decision to put a little distance between himself and Mankato solidified his management team and strengthened his company.

This somewhat laissez-faire leadership approach continues to work for Taylor Corporation today. Among its seventy-plus companies are Precision Press, Royal Stationery, Thayer Publishing, Heinrich Envelope Corporation, Schmidt Printing, and Taytronics, all Minnesota companies, none called "Taylor." "We keep different names on our companies so they have their own identity," Taylor said. "We have over fifteen thousand employees, and I hesitate to have them see themselves as one of fifteen thousand. I'd rather they see themselves as one of two hundred or one of five hundred. Then they can concentrate on their own customer base."

Taylor takes advantage of the economies of scale his large enterprise provides, but even then he doesn't force his companies to acquiesce. Taylor Corporation consolidates its purchases of inks, paper, and other supplies for all of its companies to get the best possible discounted prices. The companies are informed of the preferred suppliers and negotiated rates. "I expect them to order that unless they have some reason not to, such as it's preferable to order locally or to order from someone giving them business," Taylor said. "That's why I never say absolutely."

With more than seventy companies in seventeen states, three Canadian provinces, the United Kingdom, the Netherlands, Sweden, Australia, and Mexico, Taylor encourages local autonomy tempered by corporate direction. His division managers and company presidents provide him and his executives with a monthly written report, yet even here an uncommon flexibility exists. "I give a lot of leeway in what they write in that report," Taylor said. "They may write what they've been doing or what problems they've faced. If they are having a problem and someone's not listening, they put it in the report because they know I'm going to get it. Most try to keep it down to one page, although sometimes I get a four-page report. I see all the budgets of all the companies every month so I'm aware of what they're projecting."

Taylor Corporation has three divisions organized by how it markets to its customers: direct mail, dealer- or independent representative-based, and direct sales. "We branch out from the core of our business, usually into something our present customers want or a product we already have the distribution system or manufacturing for," Taylor said. His position on the boards of several companies helped him anticipate the softening economy that followed the Internet bubble of the late 1990s. He advised his companies to monitor their hiring more closely and directed the corporation to accumulate cash: "We're opportunists, and there are going to be great opportunities if the economy goes bad. We have a plan to grow 12 percent—it used to be 25 percent—that we put out more to get ideas on how to achieve it through internal growth, start-ups, or acquisitions."

His plan is working. Taylor Corporation is the twelfth-largest printing company in the United States, with estimated annual revenues of $1 billion. It claims 90 percent of the wedding-invitation market and dominates the markets for personalized Christmas cards, W-2 forms, company letterheads, and business cards. Yet despite building an enduring enterprise, Taylor remains a humble, self-effacing man, the quintessential Minnesotan: hardworking, modest, responsible, and just plain nice. "The secrets of success aren't secrets," he said. "They're commonsense things—you thank people, you listen to people, you show respect. And you work harder at it."

Whether he's running a multinational corporation, serving in the state Senate, working his farm, or leading the Minnesota Timberwolves, the NBA team he bought in 1995, Taylor combines the "driven" personality of a Dick Schulze with the collaborative style of a Frederick Weyerhaeuser to succeed beyond belief.

Conclusion: In a Pig's Eye

An old Yiddish proverb says, "With money in your pocket, you are wise and you are handsome and you sing well too." When we read about Minnesota's exceptional entrepreneurs, it's easy to glorify their accomplishments while overlooking the fears, mistakes, and failures that informed their decisions and shaped their destinies. We do so at our own peril, for like these entrepreneurs, we can learn from failure as well as success. And the first lesson is that everyone fails.

Few have failed more often than Ecolab's Merritt Osborn, who dealt with at least seven serious setbacks in his first fourteen years as an entrepreneur. More than once he had to have questioned the wisdom of what he was doing, fought back the fears and doubts that failure spawns, and pondered a less risky line of work. Yet he persisted, and that tenacity built an enduring enterprise.

Although no others followed the same path to success as Osborn, nearly all took perilous routes through numbing fear, debilitating mistakes, and demoralizing failure. They embraced, as Control Data's William Norris did, the words of General Douglas MacArthur, who said, "There is no such thing as security in this world. There is only opportunity."

What distinguishes these stellar Minnesota entrepreneurs is their unending desire to seize opportunity. Some saw it clearly and moved toward it purposefully. Others grabbed whatever they could reach and sifted through the possibilities for the most promising venture. Whether the vision appeared whole and compelling—what Digital River's Joel Ronning described as "connecting the dots"—or revealed itself in stages as it did for pizza maker Rose Totino, these rare entrepreneurs advanced "confidently in the direction of their dreams," as Thoreau advised, achieving "a success unexpected in common hours."

As the paths differed, so did the personalities. Outgoing people like Chun King's Jeno Paulucci, polio therapist Sister Elizabeth Kenny, and Carlson Companies' Curt Carlson excelled, as did more reserved leaders like lumber baron Frederick Weyerhaeuser and Medtronic's Earl Bakken. Some demanded full control while others delegated key responsibilities. For every J. A. O. Preus, who sought very public recognition while building Lutheran Brotherhood, there was a Glen Taylor who created a billion-dollar printing company barely visible to the public eye.

Personality, age, gender, and race had no bearing on success. Neither did the type of business or the era in which it was launched. Luck often contributed, as it did when the Merritt brothers' wagon got stuck in what turned out to be iron ore; but luck was as likely to be bad as good, as their Mountain Ore Company discovered during the financial panic of 1893. (In fact, the number of financial downturns since Minnesota became a U.S. territory, including the current bubble-bursting slowdown, suggests that this particular brand of bad luck is cyclical and possible to prepare for.)

For this book's set of entrepreneurs, the most likely predictors of success are the qualities that each, to some degree, exhibited. The first is vision.

Vision

When Cadwallader Washburn erected a flour mill for the unheard-of cost of $100,000, the people of Minneapolis and St. Anthony Falls laughed at his apparent stupidity. They laughed because they lacked Washburn's vision of a time in the near future when the growing demand for flour and production of wheat would intersect in his mill. He saw it before it happened and acted on his vision to build Washburn-Crosby into an enduring enterprise.

In Washburn's case, as it has been for many entrepreneurs in food-related businesses, the vision focuses on providing customers with a product or service they value. That value may come from a product innovation, as it did when Washburn found a way to mill spring wheat; from better delivery; or from lower costs. H. M. Byllesby of Northern States Power provided electricity cheaper and more reliably by generating it at central locations, a contrary approach that became standard industry practice. Schwan's Marvin Schwan delivered ice cream right to people's homes, a convenience people valued. Best Buy's Richard Schulze developed Concept II to differentiate his stores from the competition by giving customers a new buying experience. Glen Taylor listened to his young customers and introduced options to the wedding-invitation market, an innovation that "seems so obvious now," according to Taylor.

Pacemaker inventor Earl Bakken clarified the need for a customer focus when he wrote, "We were learning that the key to success . . . is not to build something and then hope someone will buy it, but to discover what the customer really needs and wants, then to meet or exceed the customer's expectation with both product and service."

Bakken realized the potential of a different type of vision, one that focuses on providing customers with a product or service they've never had before. Lifesaving battery-powered pacemakers did not exist until Medtronic invented them. Joel Ronning encrypted software to improve both marketing and distribution. Railroad builder James J. Hill carved out a northern route to the Pacific in the late nineteenth century; thirty years later Colonel Lewis Brittin made the same trip convenient by Northwest passenger airplanes. In between these two transportation feats, Greyhound's Carl Wickman connected cities and towns across Minnesota and around the country through regularly scheduled bus service.

The vision often blooms detailed and complete in the entrepreneur's mind, a future world so real and compelling—so obvious—that the entrepreneur cannot believe others aren't working on the same idea. While the steps to achieving the vision are often murky, the vision itself sustains the entrepreneur through the fear, anxiety, frustration, and disappointment that frequently follows.

Of course, far more people envision brilliant new products or services than actually deliver them, which suggests two more qualities that the most successful entrepreneurs possess: confidence and boldness.

Confidence

When he was seventeen, retailer George Draper Dayton bought a coal and lumberyard, bucking his parents' advice and going into debt. That same confidence emboldened him to buy a bank even though he knew nothing about banking and to take over a dry-goods company even though he had no experience managing a department store, and then to stick with it when losses soared into six figures.

As the entrepreneurs profiled in this book have shown, confidence can be a surprisingly effective substitute for knowledge. Washburn and Pillsbury started flour milling in complete ignorance of the process. Before he inherited a brewery, Theodore Hamm's only experience with beer was to drink it. J. A. O. Preus accepted a job requiring shorthand and then quickly learned it, after which he became Minnesota's commissioner of insurance and cofounder of Lutheran Brotherhood, even though no one in his family had ever owned insurance.

Tales of irrational confidence abound among these exceptional entrepreneurs. Frank Peavey believed that farming would become critical in the undeveloped west. He acted on his vision by persuading two men to become his partners selling farm implements. None of them knew anything about farm implements. The confident Peavey, later the owner of Peavey Elevator Company, was only eighteen years old.

Sister Elizabeth Kenny spent thirty years trying to convince the medical community of the superiority of her polio treatment. She relentlessly fought arrogance, ignorance, and skepticism to promote her cause. In a stunning testament to the roots of her confidence, she said, "I am right and the rest of the world is wrong." Her entrepreneurial peers would understand.

Boldness

Every successful entrepreneur must be bold, often more than once, for while it is true that great entrepreneurs begin with confidence in an uncommon vision, great companies can be built only through action. Bold action.

Northwest Airways' Colonel Lewis Brittin saw aviation as the key to Minnesota's growth. He tried to persuade individuals and groups to lead the charge, but when they would not, he said, "I'll do it myself." Brittin created an enduring enterprise out of nothing: no money, no planes, no pilots, no airmail contract, no employees. His confident action affirms Goethe's claim that "boldness has genius, power, and magic in it."

Thirty years later William Norris acted with similar disregard for rational behavior, starting a new company on the talents of a group of engineers without benefit of products, employees, facilities, or capital. He mortgaged nearly everything he owned to invest in Control Data.

James J. Hill risked everything he had to buy the St. Paul and Pacific railroad in the fourth year of a stubborn economic depression. Several years later Frederick Weyerhaeuser paid Hill $5.4 million for timber in the Northwest, although the means to harvest and market it had not been devised.

Curt Carlson discussed his idea for grocery-store trading stamps with a professor, a banker, his parents, and his wife, and they all told him to forget it. Nobody else had tried it and the Great Depression had only recently released its grip on the nation. If it were such a great idea, they surely figured, somebody would have done it already. Keep the stable job, they advised. Instead, Carlson boldly pursued his vision for Gold Bond stamps.

Such boldness distinguishes every entrepreneur listed in this book. All faced significant risk. All acted boldly rather than walk away or hedge their bets. In many cases they took a "calculated and managed risk," as Best Buy's Dick Schulze described it, but sometimes they just jumped. Poet Guillaume Apollinaire captures the powerful internal voice that compelled these entrepreneurs to act:

> Come to the edge, he said.
> They said: We are afraid.
> Come to the edge, he said.
> They came.
> He pushed them . . . and they flew.

Many new ventures flew because of qualities that took the teeth out of the most fearsome risks: innovation, experience, and teamwork.

Innovation

What if?

What if software could be encrypted and put on a disk?

What if we expanded our product lines to create an electronics superstore?

What if we put the vegetables in one can and the meat in another and call it a Divider-Pak?

What if grocers used trading stamps to build their businesses?

What if we created a regular bus schedule for the towns we serve?

What if we had a northern route to the Pacific?

Innovation energizes vision. No entrepreneur would take the risks and make the sacrifices for an uninspiring vision, and no vision is inspiring without innovation. A new product or service. A better way of doing things. An approach no one has thought of or executed before.

The most obvious innovations involve products or services that previously did not exist: William McKnight and 3M's waterproof sandpaper and cellophane tape; Osborn and Ecolab's carpet cleaner and dishwasher detergent; Hans Andersen and Andersen Windows' "two-bundle" frames; Bakken and Medtronic's pacemakers; and Ronning and Digital River's software distribution. Being first grants an entrepreneur unrivaled access to virgin territory, whether it's the first newspaper in St. Paul, the first airline in Minnesota, or the first pacemaker in the world.

In today's Internet world, being first can also mean being funded. "Raw technology that changes the fundamentals of how things are done will continue to be funded," said Ronning, "but concepts aren't being funded anymore."

Fortunately, innovation is not limited to raw technology. Frederick Weyerhaeuser's innovation was to use his skills as a negotiator to unite independent sawmill owners. Land O'Lakes' John Brandt applied similar skills to persuade individual creameries to become part of a larger and more influential cooperative.

For some the innovation is internal, a way to work more efficiently and serve more effectively. W. W. Mayo and his sons William and Charles promoted innovative systems that enabled their clinic to flourish. William McKnight allowed 3M employees to devote some of their time to tinkering with new ideas, an approach that produced Scotch tape, Post-It notes, and a culture that values innovation.

Among today's business leaders a new performance measure has emerged: percent of revenues from products introduced in the last three or four years. They recognize that, whether a company is new or established, innovation continues to energize vision and drive growth.

Experience

A single word cannot adequately describe the range of backgrounds upon which successful entrepreneurs launched their companies. Northern States Power's H. M. Byllesby, for example, spent his entire working life on electricity. He worked for Thomas Edison and George Westinghouse. He designed an entire electrical station. He invented more than forty electric lighting devices. He ran a subsidiary of an electric company. By the time he decided to start his own utility, he had twenty-eight years of experience to guide him.

Leeann Chin spent a lifetime learning about Chinese cooking. As an adult she discovered how to turn her love of cooking into a business, first by developing managerial skills in her sewing and alterations business and then by honing her customer skills by teaching cooking and catering parties and receptions.

James J. Hill worked for or around railroads for nearly twenty years before launching the Great Northern, but his experience was not limited to railroads. He worked for a steamboat company, pressed and sold hay, worked in a warehouse, and ran a coal-fuel business. During the Civil War he learned how to buy and sell goods at a profit and moved products inexpensively. His time at steamboat companies and railroads taught him the fundamentals of transportation, wholesale merchandising, commodity trading, and logistics. By the time he bought his own railroad, he was well prepared to move boldly toward his dreams.

Several Minnesota entrepreneurs built enduring enterprises upon experiences that had little or nothing to do with their eventual businesses. Cadwallader Washburn was first a politician. Theodore Hamm was a butcher. Colonel Lewis Brittin managed a railroad terminal. The Merritt brothers were loggers. That they were able to apply these experiences to entirely new ventures speaks to the intelligence and adaptability they possessed.

John MacMillan of W. W. Cargill Company paid for his early experiences when, at the age of twenty-two, he and his brothers built and ran grain elevators in Texas. A financial panic and grasshopper plague threatened the survival of their fledgling business, but they hung on for five years. Reflecting on the difficult times, MacMillan wrote, "My character is broadening and hardening under such a stress of experience. My judgment is growing keener and my powers of observation and reason stronger and the day will yet come when all I have suffered will prove a powerful lever to aid in ultimate success." Seven years after closing his Texas business MacMillan took over Cargill's grain business. His early experiences helped him transform the company into an international leader.

Young entrepreneurs tend to chafe at the need for experience, but Joel Ronning and the survival of Digital River attest to its value in any industry. As Curt Carlson wrote, "I would strongly urge every young man or woman with entrepreneurial stirrings to do what I did: spend some time learning from an already successful enterprise what the business world is all about."

One of the lessons such an experience teaches is that no entrepreneur has to know everything about everything. Experts abound, and the wise entrepreneur learns how to weave them into his or her vision, adding the knowledge and skills a new enterprise demands.

Teamwork

We tend to think of entrepreneurs as lone riders. To the degree that an entrepreneur creates something out of nothing, that perception is true. What it misses, however, is the essential contribution of every entrepreneur's team.

Sometimes that team is family, as it was for the Fullers, Mayos, Cargills, MacMillans, Hills, Daytons, Andersens, and Osborns. As it was for the "seven iron men." Other times it is an inseparable partner: Washburn and George Christian, Hamm and Jacob Schmidt, McKnight and Archibald Bush, Brittin and "Speed" Holman, Preus and Herman Ekern, Bakken and Palmer Hermundslie.

With rare exceptions, one person in each of these examples stands alone as the entrepreneur who launched an enduring enterprise. The rarest exception is the team of Jimmy Jam Harris and Terry Lewis, partners in a vision of what their music-production company would be, in the path they chose to realize that vision, and in the accolades and profits their enterprise has produced. A 50-50 split. No contract required.

Sister Antonia McHugh exemplified the truest brand of teamwork, inspiring her teachers to pursue advanced degrees, taking each in turn on her travels, and teaching them about the world beyond their college. She made those around her smarter, more confident, and more capable, knowing that her vision for the College of St. Catherine could not be achieved alone.

Theodore Hamm felt so strongly about his employees' needs that he actually encouraged them to form a union. The fact that they then elected him to be their first president suggests a heartfelt sense of team.

Hans Andersen built Andersen Windows on a philosophy of teamwork formed in the first English words he learned: "All together, boys." When told that the men he had brought from St. Cloud to work at a Hudson sawmill would be laid off, he quit the mill, opened a lumberyard, and hired the workers. Eleven years after he started manufacturing windows he decided to share the wealth his growing business was generating. His plan involved paying the best wages in the industry, setting a reasonable percent of the profits for investors, and sharing the rest of the profits with his employees. By his actions Andersen affirmed the value he placed on every member of his team.

Glen Taylor calls this "common-sense things: You thank people, you listen to people, you show respect." In return the entrepreneur gains knowledge he or she lacks, the exceptional skills of others, and the camaraderie inspired by working together to build something important and lasting.

Such camaraderie is especially valuable when a new enterprise stumbles. No entrepreneur escapes adversity. The best learn from it, overcome it, and build on it, a skill that requires exceptional tenacity.

Tenacity

When Jeno Paulucci decided to start his own business, he chose to sell something he knew: garlic. The company failed when the demand for garlic never materialized, leaving Paulucci heavily in debt. A stream of formidable obstacles followed, including bank rejection, labor unrest, client dissatisfaction, a lawsuit, fire, loss of partner, IRS investigation, and packaging problems. It would have been understandable if Paulucci had given up at some point in this torturous journey. Others have quit after enduring much less. But he persevered because he had learned tenacity as a child, scavenging for coal over mining officials' objections and prying up wood paving blocks for fuel to heat the family home. He had witnessed how bosses had taken advantage of his father and decided to be his own boss. And he refused to let any obstacle beat him. "You have to have an unquenchable appetite for success," he said. "The entrepreneur is always reaching for new challenges."

Too often the challenges reach out and grab the entrepreneur, from natural disasters such as insect plagues and tornadoes to economic declines to the problems that beset any business. The tenacious entrepreneurs who weather these storms discover, as Nietzsche said, "What does not destroy me makes me strong."

Two hours after Cadwallader Washburn arrived in Minneapolis to assess the damage caused by an explosion at one of his mills, he stepped off the dimensions for a new flour mill amid the debris. Within a year production recovered and within two it doubled.

Red Wing Shoe Company's Charles Beckman walked away from a train wreck and continued his sales trip rather than returning home.

Leading experts in the medical community repeatedly warned Sister Elizabeth Kenny that her methods of treating polio patients were unscientific and ineffective. Such relentless repudiation from esteemed doctors would have silenced most, especially if they lacked formal medical training, but it did not stop Sister Kenny. Her resolve to help patients only intensified, as did her disdain for most physicians. A Cornell Medical College doctor once said something she didn't like and she countered, "Dr. Stimson knows nothing about the early treatment of polio except what I taught him, and there is still quite a bit he doesn't know."

Sister Kenny called it "bulldog courage." Leeann Chin demonstrated bulldog courage when she opened a restaurant against all advice and then overcame the failure of her ovens on her first day and a loss of electrical power on her second. Ecolab's Merritt Osborn exhibited bulldog courage when he persisted in building an enduring enterprise through the failure of four businesses, the effort to market new products, and the struggle to find potential investors.

One of Minnesota's first great entrepreneurs summarized it best, for men and women alike. "Men of the right stamp will always find the right spot," said newspaper founder James Madison Goodhue, "and men of the right *nerve* will stay in them and flourish, regardless of all temporary inconvenience." Goodhue stepped off a steamboat onto Minnesota soil in the spring of 1849. Walking along dirt roads through the ramshackle houses of his new home, he learned that the tiny community had only recently been called St. Paul after the erection of a Catholic church, a name much preferred over the one it replaced. Eleven years before Goodhue's arrival, Canadian voyageur Pierre Parrant claimed land on what would become St. Paul. Parrant had both an entrepreneurial spirit and a distinctive physical feature. The spirit moved him to open a grocery store and bar. The feature, one eye in the shape of a pig's eye, became both his nickname and the community's name when somebody sent a letter from his store with the return address of "Pig's Eye."

The entrepreneurs featured in this book, from Goodhue to Taylor, would not have let a name like Pig's Eye impede their plans. Despite far greater obstacles they built enduring enterprises beyond anyone's imagination. They transformed vision into reality by moving boldly and confidently in the direction of their dreams. They created value for their customers. They learned from their experiences. They found strength in those who joined their quest. They conquered adversity.

And ultimately, they succeeded.

Bibliography

A Fuller Life: The Story of H. B. Fuller Company. St. Paul: H. B. Fuller Company, 1986.

"About ASCAP." American Society of Composers, Authors, and Publishers, http://www.ascap.com/about/harris-bio.html. March 21, 2001.

Bakken, Earl E. *One Man's Full Life.* Minneapolis: Medtronic, Inc., 1999.

Beck, Bill. *Northern Lights: An Illustrated History of Minnesota Power.* Duluth, Minnesota: Minnesota Power, 1986.

Berthel, Mary Wheelhouse. *Horns of Thunder: The Life and Times of James M. Goodhue, including Selections from His Writings.* St. Paul: Minnesota Historical Society, 1948.

Blegen, Theodore C. *Minnesota: A History of the State.* Minneapolis: University of Minnesota Press, 1975.

Borger, Judith Yates. "It Began When L. P. Ordway Bought 3M—for $14,000." *Twin Cities* 5, no 10, 25, October 1982.

Brissett, Liz. "Social and Industrial Upheavals Mark 1910s." *100 Years of Minnesota Business. CityBusiness, Corporate Report, and Minnesota Ventures,* 28, December 1999.

Broehl, Wayne G. Jr. *Cargill: Trading the World's Grain.* Hanover and London: University Press of New England, 1992.

Carlson, Curtis L. *Good as Gold: The Story of the Carlson Companies.* Minneapolis: Carlson Companies, 1994.

Clark, Clifford E. Jr. *Minnesota in a Century of Change: The State and Its People Since 1900.* St. Paul: Minnesota Historical Society Press, 1989.

Cohn, Victor. *Sister Kenny: The Woman Who Challenged the Doctors.* Minneapolis: University of Minnesota Press, 1975.

Collopy, Anne M. "A Woman for Today: Mother Antonia McHugh." Slide-show transcript. College of St. Catherine, St. Paul, Minnesota, 1973.

Dayton, George Draper. *George Draper Dayton: An Autobiography.* Private printing, 1933.

De Kruif, Paul. *Seven Iron Men.* New York: Harcourt, Brace and Company, 1929.

Druskoff, Mark. "Iron Man." *Minnesota Business* 10, no 3, 44, July 2000.

Edgar, William C. *The Medal of Gold.* Minneapolis: The Bellman Company, 1925.

"Executives of the Decade." *Twin Cities Business Monthly* 6, no 1, 37, September 1998.

Fiedler, Terry. "Soul of a Billionaire." *Star Tribune,* April 26, 1998.

The First Forty Years. St. Paul: Economics Laboratory, Inc., 1984.

Flanagan, John T. *Theodore Hamm in Minnesota: His Family and Brewery.* St. Paul: Pogo Press, 1989.

Gelbach, Deborah L. *From This Land: A History of Minnesota's Empires, Enterprises, and Entrepreneurs.* Northridge, California: Windsor Publications, 1988.

Grant, Tina, ed. *International Directory of Company Histories.* Vol. 23. Chicago: St. James Press, 1998.

Hakala Associates, Inc. *A Common Bond: The Story of Lutheran Brotherhood.* Minneapolis: Lutheran Brotherhood, 1989.

Hallett, Anthony, and Diane Hallett. *Encyclopedia of Entrepreneurs.* New York: John Wiley and Sons, 1997.

Harris, Moira F. *Louise's Legacy: Hamm Family Stories.* St. Paul: Pogo Press, 1998.

Hatcher, Harlan. *A Century of Iron and Men.* Indianapolis: Bobbs-Merrill, 1950.

Heilbron, Bertha Lion. *The Thirty-Second State: A Pictorial History of Minnesota.* St. Paul: Minnesota Historical Society, 1966.

Hidy, Ralph W., Frank Ernest Hill, and Allan Nevins. *Timber and Men: The Weyerhaeuser Story.* New York: Macmillan, 1963.

Holcombe, Major R. I., and William H. Bingham, eds. *Compendium of History and Biography of Minneapolis and Hennepin County, Minnesota.* Chicago: Henry Taylor and Co., 1914.

Huck, Virginia. *Brand of the Tartan: The 3M Story.* New York: Appleton-Century-Crofts, 1955.

Ingersoll, Paul Baughman. *The Merritt Brothers and the Opening of the Mesaba Iron Range.* Chicago: University of Chicago, 1928.

Jean, Sheryl. "Minnesota Economy Soars—Until the Crash." *100 Years of Minnesota Business. CityBusiness, Corporate Report, and Ventures,* 40, December 1999.

Kaplan, Anne R., and Marilyn Ziebarth, eds. *Making Minnesota Territory: 1849–1858.* St. Paul: Minnesota Historical Society Press, 1999.

Keillor, Steven J. *Cooperative Commonwealth: Co-ops in Rural Minnesota, 1859–1939.* St. Paul: Minnesota Historical Society Press, 2000.

Kennelly, Sister Karen. "The Dynamic Sister Antonia and the College of St. Catherine." *Ramsey County History* 14, no 1, 3, 1978.

Kunz, Virginia Brainard, ed. *Ramsey County History* 24, no 2, 3, 1989.

Kurschner, Dale. "Best Buy Harder." *Corporate Report Minnesota* 28, no 8, 66, August 1997.

Lass, William E. *Minnesota: A History.* New York: W. W. Norton and Company, 1998.

Lassen, Tina. "Straight Shooter!" *Northwest Airlines World Traveler.*

Leipold, L. E. *Jeno F. Paulucci, Merchant Philanthropist.* Minneapolis: T. S. Denison and Company, 1968.

Lillard, Richard G. "Timber King." *The Pacific Spectator: A Journal of Interpretation* (Winter 1947).

Lisanti, Tony, ed. "Building a New Empire." *DSN Retailing Today* 40, no 1A, 7, January 2001.

MacMillan, W. Duncan, with Patricia Condon Johnston. *MacMillan: The American Grain Family.* Afton, Minnesota: Afton Historical Society Press, 1998.

Martin, Albro. *James J. Hill and the Opening of the Northwest.* St. Paul: Minnesota Historical Society Press, 1976.

Martyka, Jim. "Women and Minorities Make Workplace Gains." *100 Years of Minnesota Business. CityBusiness, Corporate Report, and Ventures,* 86, December 1999.

Marvin, Patrice Avon, and Nicholas Curchin Vrooman. *Heart and Sole: A Story of the Red Wing Shoe Company.* Red Wing, Minnesota: Red Wing Shoe Company, 1986.

Mayo, Charles W. *Mayo: The Story of My Family and My Career.* Garden City, New York: Doubleday, 1968.

McAdams, Janine. "Jimmy and Terry's Excellent Venture." *Billboard* 104, no 50, JL3, December 12, 1992.

Meier, Peg. *Bring Warm Clothes: Letters and Photos from Minnesota's Past.* Minneapolis: Neighbors Publishing, 1981.

Milton, John W. "How 15 Minnesota Businesses Got Their Start." *100 Years of Minnesota Business. City Business, Corporate Report, and Ventures,* 94, December 1999.

Morgan, Dan. *Merchants of Grain.* New York: Viking Press, 1979.

Niemela, Jennifer. "Limping Economy Rebounds, Levels Off." *100 Years of Minnesota Business. CityBusiness, Corporate Report, and Ventures,* 66, December 1999.

Novak, Jay. "Executive of the Year." *Corporate Report Minnesota* 18, no 1, 53, January 1987.

100 Years of Trust: 1884–1984. Minneapolis: Northrup King Company, 1984.

Operations Manual—Food, Beverage and Guest Service, Leeann Chin Chinese Cuisine, November 2000, 2.

Parsons, Martha. "Workers Organize during State's Hard Times." *100 Years of Minnesota Business. CityBusiness, Corporate Report, and Ventures,* 50, December 1999.

Pederson, Jay P., ed. *International Directory of Company Histories.* Vol. 30. Chicago: St. James Press, 2000.

———. *International Directory of Company Histories.* Vol. 36. Chicago: St. James Press, 2001.

Pile, Robert B. *Top Entrepreneurs and Their Businesses.* Minneapolis: The Oliver Press, 1993.

———. *Women Business Leaders.* Minneapolis: The Oliver Press, 1995.

Pine, Carol. *Northern States People: The Past 70 Years.* St. Paul: North Central Publishing, 1979.

Pine, Carol, and Susan Mundale. *Self-made: The Stories of 12 Minnesota Entrepreneurs.* Minneapolis: Dorn Books, 1982.

Powell, William J. *Pillsbury's Best: A Company History from 1869.* Minneapolis: Pillsbury Company, 1985.

Regan, Shawn. "Post-War Boom Includes Babies, Spending." *100 Years of Minnesota Business. CityBusiness, Corporate Minnesota, and Ventures,* 76, December 1999.

Reynolds, Nood Wharton. *Minnesota: Land of Lakes and Innovation.* Encino, California: Cherbo Publishing Group, 1998.

Richards, Bill. "Your Career Matters: Risk-Taker Cashes in on His Retail Mistakes." *The Wall Street Journal Europe,* September 26, 2000, 32.

Ruble, Kenneth D. *Flight to the Top.* New York: Viking Press, 1986.

————. *The Magic Circle.* Bayport, Minnesota: Andersen Corporation, 1978.

————. *The Peavey Story.* Minneapolis: Peavey Company, 1963.

Schafer, Lee. "Richard Schulze's Manifest Destiny." *Corporate Report Minnesota* 26, no 3, 26, March 1995.

Schisgall, Oscar. *The Greyhound Story: From Hibbing to Everywhere.* Chicago: J. G. Ferguson Publishing Company, 1985.

Schouweiler, Sara, and A. N. Sandt. *Fifty Years of Red Wing Shoes.* Red Wing, Minnesota: Red Wing Shoe Company, 1955.

Smith, Shawnee. "Jam & Lewis Are Still in Flyte." *Billboard* 44t, January 24, 1998.

Stevens, John H. *Recollections of James M. Goodhue.* Read before the Minnesota Editorial Association, February 1864. St. Paul: Pioneer Press Company, vol. 6, 1894.

Swanson, William. *Minneapolis: City of Enterprise, Center of Excellence.* Minneapolis: Windsor Publications, 1989.

Walker, David A. *Iron Frontier: The Discovery and Early Development of Minnesota's Three Ranges.* St. Paul: Minnesota Historical Society Press, 1979.

Weimer, De'Ann. "The Houdini of Consumer Electronics." *Business Week,* no 3583, 67, June 22, 1998.

Weintraub, Adam. "Decade Sees Rise of 'Empire Builders.'" *100 Years of Minnesota Business.* CityBusiness, Corporate Report, and Ventures, 18, December 1999.

White, Willmon L. *The Ultra Entrepreneur.* Phoenix: Gullers Pictorial, 1988.

Worthy, James C. *William C. Norris: A Portrait of a Maverick.* Cambridge, Massachusetts: Ballinger Publishing Company, 1987.

Index

Created by Eileen Quam

Stephen George has been writing company histories and other types of business communication for more than twenty-five years. As a writer and consultant, he has helped twenty organizations integrate the Baldrige management model and has written four books on the subject.

Marilyn Carlson Nelson is the chair and CEO of the Carlson Companies, a business founded in 1938 by her father, Minnesota native and entrepreneur Curt Carlson.